SUCCESSFUL CUSTOMER SERVICE

PAULINE ROWSON

Viva Books

New Delhi | Mumbai | Chennai | Kolkata | Bangalore | Hyderabad | Kochi | Guwahati

First Indian Edition 2010
Reprinted 2013

VIVA BOOKS PRIVATE LIMITED

- 4737/23 Ansari Road, Daryaganj, New Delhi 110 002
  E-mail: vivadelhi@vivagroupindia.net, Tel. 42242200
- 76, Service Industries, Shirvane, Sector 1, Nerul, Navi Mumbai 400 706
  E-mail: vivamumbai@vivagroupindia.net, Tel. 27721273, 27721274
- Jamals Fazal Chambers, 26 Greams Road, Chennai 600 006
  E-mail: vivachennai@vivagroupindia.net, Tel. 28290304, 28294241
- B-103, Jindal Towers, 21/1A/3 Darga Road, Kolkata 700 017
  E-mail: vivakolkata@vivagroupindia.net, Tel. 22836381, 22816713
- 7, Sovereign Park Apartments, 56-58, K. R. Road, Basavanagudi, Bangalore 560 004
  E-mail: vivabangalore@vivagroupindia.net, Tel. 26607409, 26607410
- 101-102 Mughal Marc Apartments, 3-4-637 to 641, Narayanguda, Hyderabad 500 029
  E-mail: vivahyderabad@vivagroupindia.net, Tel. 27564481, 27564482
- Beevi Towers, First Floor, SRM Road, Kaloor, Kochi 682 018, Kerala
  E-mail: vivakochi@vivagroupindia.net, Tel: 0484-2403055, 2403056
- 232, GNB Road, Beside UCO Bank, Silpukhuri, Guwahati 781 003
  E-mail: vivaguwahati@vivagroupindia.net, Tel: 0361-2666386

www.vivagroupindia.com

Published by arrangement with

Crimson Publishing,
a division of Crimson Business Ltd
Westminster House, Kew Road
Richmond, Surrey TW9 2ND

ISBN : 978-81-309-1502-9

Published by Vinod Vasishtha for Viva Books Private Limited, 4737/23, Ansari Road, Daryaganj, New Delhi - 110 002.

Printed and bound by Raj Press, R-3, Inderpuri, New Delhi - 110 012.

CONTENTS

PAULINE ROWSON

Pauline Rowson lives in the UK and has helped countless organisations to improve their customer service skills. She is author of several marketing and self-help books and for many years ran her own successful marketing, PR and training company. She is a popular speaker at conferences and workshops and is also the author of the popular marine mystery series of crime and thriller novels.

INTRODUCTION

WARNING SIGNS

How often have you heard remarks like this?

> 'You're the fifth person to complain about that today!'
> 'Everyone moans about that'
> 'We can't *possibly* do *that*'
> 'If it's not on the shelf we haven't got it'
> 'I'll put you on hold...'

Sound familiar? I expect you've got many more examples of poor customer service from all types of businesses: solicitors to IT companies, public sector organisations to the medical profession, plumbers, builders, banks, butchers, bakers and candlestick makers. If you're in business you have customers: whether they are called patients, clients, or passengers they are all CUSTOMERS. They hand over their money to you in exchange for a product or a service.

You are my customer. You have parted with your money and purchased this book. You have certain expectations from this book. If it disappoints you, then you become a dissatisfied customer. Where did you purchase this book? Was it on the internet or in a bookshop? What was the service like? Will you buy a book from that organisation again? If not, why not?

Having a good reputation for excellent service and products is one very successful way of building a competitive advantage for your business. But be warned, a good reputation is not easy to attain, or retain. This book will show you how you can develop a customer service policy that can help your organisation deliver successful customer service.

It is often weak management and poor communication that results in poor customer service. The first section of the book, therefore, examines how you can develop a successful customer service policy, motivate your staff and improve communications within your organisation. The second section looks at the interpersonal skills needed by individuals for delivering good customer service.

WHAT THIS BOOK COVERS:

- How good customer relations can help you win more business
- How to win more business by retaining customers and gaining recommendations from them
- How to satisfy your customers' needs
- How to develop an effective customer service policy
- How to use positive behaviour and attitude to win more business
- How to build a better rapport with your customers
- How to handle anger, complaints and difficult customers and turn them into satisfied customers

PART 1

CREATING A CULTURE OF EXCELLENT CUSTOMER SERVICE

CHAPTER 1

Why good customer service is essential

Why provide good customer service?

Providing excellent customer service consistently is not an easy task but if we don't give our customers what they need and want, and we don't deliver it in a way that is acceptable to them, or indeed in a manner that exceeds their expectations, then we will lose them. This chapter examines some elements of poor customer service and why providing excellent customer service is essential to the success of an organisation.

EXAMINING YOUR OWN CUSTOMER SERVICE

First, let's start with a simple questionnaire. Tick the answer you think is correct.

1. What is your opinion of the following?
   - ❑ a) It's only front line staff that deal with customers in our organisation.
   - ❑ b) We don't really have customers.
   - ❑ c) Everybody has a customer.

2. What do you think about the service in your organisation?
   - ❑ a) The quality of service inside the organisation is just as important as outside.
   - ❑ b) How we serve the public is the most important issue.
   - ❑ c) Service isn't really something we think about, it just happens.

3. How do you feel about the following?
   - ❑ a) Other departments can think what they like about this department, I don't really care.
   - ❑ b) I care what other departments think about our department, but I have no control over it.
   - ❑ c) I am responsible for what other departments think about our department.

4. What do you think about people's behaviour?
   - ❑ a) It is directly affected by the treatment they receive.
   - ❑ b) People behave the way they want to regardless of the treatment they receive.
   - ❑ c) Only some people's behaviour is affected by the way they are treated.

5. Which do you think is the correct statement?
   - ❑ a) Customer care is all about smiling at the customer.
   - ❑ b) Customer care is about meeting customers' needs.
   - ❑ c) Customer care is only necessary if you work in a shop.

6. Does your behaviour with colleagues have anything to do with the quality of the service you give external customers?
   - ❑ a) Not really.
   - ❑ b) It has some effect.
   - ❑ c) It has everything to do with it.

You might also like to give this questionnaire to your staff.

Now let's see how well you and/or your staff understand what providing good customer service is about.

Here are the correct answers:

1. What is your opinion of the following?
   c) Everybody has a customer.

2. What do you think about the service in your organisation?
   a) The quality of service inside the organisation is just as important as outside.

3. How do you feel about the following?
   c) I am responsible for what other departments think about our department.

4. What do you think about people's behaviour?
   a) It is directly affected by the treatment they receive.

5. Which do you think is the correct statement?
   b) Customer care is about meeting customers' needs.

6. Does your behaviour with colleagues have anything to do with the quality of the service you give external customers?
   c) It has everything to do with it.

Are you and your staff already customer friendly or at least on the right lines by getting the correct answers to the questionnaire, or do you have some considerable way to go yet? If you do need to improve then the following chapters will help you.

WINNING MORE BUSINESS FROM EXISTING CUSTOMERS

Marketing strategies within organisations are often geared towards winning new business from new customers. This is all very well but what about winning more business from your existing customers? They are, after all, the easiest people to sell to, but time after time they are ignored.

Many organisations fail to realise the value of their existing customers, or the fact that they can sell more to them. They treat them in a cavalier manner, often ignoring them once the business is won, and in some cases making it as difficult as possible for customers to purchase products or services. It sometimes amazes me that businesses make any money at all. Of course some don't and subsequently fail. Many organisations chase the Holy Grail of obtaining new customers, spending time, money and energy on capturing them only to provide them with a service or product that quite frankly is inferior. What a waste.

If we do not look after our customers then someone else will. In addition, those dissatisfied customers will tell others about their awful experience with you. Once you have a negative reputation it is extremely difficult to reverse. Because of the speed, ease of use, increased access and global reach of the internet, bad news travels almomst as fast as the speed of light. So, once a negative remark is on the internet it is there for all to see, thereby further damaging your organisations reputation.

It is generally said that:

96% of dissatisfied customers do not go back and complain

But they do tell 7 other people how bad you are*

13% will tell at least 20 others*

90% will never return

It costs 8 times as much to attract a new customer as it does to keep an existing one

(*The internet vastly increases this amount. If the customer hasn't told you what's wrong but has posted a negative comment on the internet it will remain there, spreading the bad news.)

With those kind of figures isn't it foolish not to get things right inside your organisation?

So what goes wrong?

There are several things that can and do go wrong within an organisation.

ACTION POINT

Think for a moment of all the things that annoy you when you are a customer.

Now draw up a list.

If you employ staff then get them to do the same. You could organise them into groups and put all the elements that annoy them as customers on a flip chart or white board.

Now look at my list below – is it very similar to yours, or do you have some additional points?

Here are some of the things that annoy me as a customer:

- Being passed around
- People not returning calls
- Having to chase up all the time
- People not taking ownership of the problem
- Obvious insincerity
- Poor communication of mistakes and problems
- Being kept waiting
- Voice mail and music whilst on hold
- The telephonist never coming back to you
- Staff not knowing enough about who does what
- Staff making mistakes – again and again
- Arrogance and complacency
- Rigid inflexible procedures
- Being patronised
- Staff who couldn't care less/are rude/lacking in product knowledge
- Not delivering on time!

And sadly there are many more...

ACTION POINT

Now examine the list you and your staff have compiled.

Ask yourself if any of these things are happening in your organisation.

Can you honestly say, with hand on heart, that these things *never* happen?

I bet you can't. Of course things do go wrong; after all, we are only human. But there are some mistakes that are made time and time again. It is these that you need to identify and resolve. And if your staff have a 'couldn't care less' attitude then you need to ask how motivated are they? How motivated are you?

If you are a supervisor, manager or director then it is your responsibility to motivate and enthuse the staff and to put into place procedures that ensure the best possible customer service is delivered – consistently.

Here are some further questions you need to ask yourself:

ACTION POINT

1. How close are you to front line staff – those who deal with the customer on a daily basis?
2. If you are based in a head office rather than at the heart of the customer operations, or in an office remote from where the customer is dealt with, then do you honestly know what the problems are?
3. How often do you spend time on the 'shop floor' or on the front desk?
4. Is your visit announced to the staff and therefore they are ready and on their 'best behaviour' for you? Or do you often drop in unannounced to see for yourself exactly how things are handled on a daily basis?
5. Do you see the letters or emails of complaints, or handle telephone calls from disgruntled customers? Or is this dealt with by someone else and you never get to review them or hear about them?
6. How often do you survey or talk to your customers and ask them for their feedback?

Just examining, or even considering, the answers to the above questions can give you some indication of whether or not you are really in touch with your customers and if you know what problems exist. And you need to know, because if you don't then how are you ever going to be able to put things right?

TOP TIPS

Encouraging your customers to complain or at least to give you feedback is the best that can happen. The worse is that they say nothing.

Not knowing what problems your customers face is far more damaging for your organisation because it never gives you the opportunity to correct what is wrong, therefore allowing even more customers to experience the same problems, creating more missed sales for your organisation and damaging your reputation.

The causes of poor customer service

Poor communication is often at the heart of poor customer service. In large organisations this becomes even more pronounced as layers of management prevent problems from being recognised, accepted and rectified. But small organisations are also at fault. Along with poor communication as one of the causes of poor customer service, are weak and ineffective management and disaffected and demotivated staff.

> Providing good customer service is essential for the survival and success of your business.

WHAT IS 'GOOD' CUSTOMER SERVICE?

Well, it's not just about smiling at the customer and saying, 'Have a nice day.' As you will see from this book, it goes much deeper. Providing excellent customer service is a philosophy, a complete way of doing business. Delivering exceptional customer service is a complex, onerous and never-ending task, but its rewards can be huge in terms of job satisfaction, motivated staff and increased profits.

Providing excellent customer service **consistently** is not easy, far from it. Why? Because **people** deliver customer services, **people** make products and provide a service, and **people** are fallible.

We all have different personalities, varying degrees of confidence, and diverse styles of communication. We have good days and bad days. We have moods, headaches and heartaches, and all these affect how we perform and interact with others. Is it no wonder that we can sometimes get it wrong!

Your challenge as a manager, director or owner of an organisation is to minimise these problems, eliminate the scope for error, and provide guidelines and rules to help people perform in a manner that will satisfy your customers. Above all ***you*** need to **set an example** (even when ***you*** have a headache!)

TOP TIPS

Good customer service starts at the top of the organisation.

WHY GOOD CUSTOMER SERVICE IS IMPORTANT

We've already seen what a dissatisfied customer can do for your sales and profit levels – it can send them plummeting. So what can a satisfied customer do?

- Satisfied customers become – advocates
- Satisfied customers become – repeat purchasers
- Satisfied customers bring you – prospects (who in turn become customers)
- Satisfied customers increase your sales and profits

By winning the loyalty of your customers you can increase sales for your organisation.

TOP TIPS

Word of mouth recommendation is a very powerful and highly cost effective marketing tool.

And if you're still not convinced that providing good customer service is essential to your business here are 12 more reasons why you should take the time to get this right.

12 benefits of providing good customer service

1. Increased revenue
2. Increased efficiency
3. Less waste
4. Improved staff morale and confidence
5. Reduction in staff turnover and absenteeism
6. Saves money
7. Enables individuals to take responsibility – saves time
8. Increased customer confidence – which leads to more purchases
9. Gives employees a sense of pride in the company – increased motivation
10. Increased profits
11. Happier shareholders (if you have them)
12. Less bad publicity, more good publicity, which in turn brings in more customers

Plus there is another overwhelming and compelling reason for providing excellent customer service – it can give you an edge on your competitors.

In order to provide excellent customer service, you and your staff need to develop good interpersonal skills. This means you need to be able to:

- Listen and interpret needs accurately
- Ask the right questions
- Have a positive attitude
- Be tactful and helpful
- Have an open mind about people
- Have good self esteem
- Be quick thinking
- Have an assertive manner
- Be approachable and well mannered
- Have excellent communication skills
- Be a good team player
- Have good body language and a presentable appearance

You also need to understand three vital things:

1. **Who your customers are**
2. **What they want from you**
3. **Why they buy from you**

The following chapters will help you to:

- Analyse your market
- Draw up and implement a customer service policy
- Provide you with some interpersonal skills to help you deliver that excellent customer service

We are not born with these interpersonal skills already fully developed. They need to be learnt and then practised. Often we develop many of these skills as children, learning from our parents, guardians, teachers and others. But dealing with the public on a continuous basis is no easy task, and particularly when under pressure or handling the difficult customer or a sensitve situation. Many of us will require additional and ongoing training to help us become and stay assertive to improve our connumincation skills and to show us how to interpret and use the most appropriate body language.

QUICK RECAP

- *If you don't look after your customers then someone else will.*
- *Dissatisfied customers will tell others about their awful experience with you.*
- *Once you have a negative reputation it is extremely difficult to reverse it.*
- *Providing good customer service is essential for the survival and success of your business.*
- *Delivering exceptional customer service can reap rewards in terms of job satisfaction, motivated staff and increased profits.*
- *Satisfied customers become advocates and repeat purchasers, and recommend you to others.*
- *Excellent customer service can give you an edge on your competitors.*
- *You and your staff need to develop good interpersonal skills.*
- *You need to put in place a good customer service policy.*

CHAPTER 2

Knowing your customers

The more you know about your customers the more successful you will be in delivering the kind of exceptional service they require. But this isn't as straightforward as it seems because you may have many different groups of customers all with different needs. This chapter examines who your customers really are, what they buy and why they buy.

WHO ARE YOUR CUSTOMERS AND WHAT DO THEY WANT?

Quite often organisations see their customers as only the group of people who *buy* their products or services but it goes much deeper than this. There are many different groups of 'customers' within or surrounding an organisation who have a vested interested in it or demands upon it.

EXAMPLE

A local newspaper, its customers are:

- *Readers (people who pay to buy the newspaper or pass it on to others to read)*
- *Advertisers (people who pay to advertise in the newspaper)*
- *Shareholders (who want a return on their investment)*
- *Councils and other local organisations (who wish to inform local people)*
- *Newsagents (who sell the newspaper to readers)*
- *Regulatory bodies (who need to make sure the newspaper is complying with laws)*
- *Suppliers (who sell goods to the newspaper company)*
- *Staff (who work for the newspaper)*

Although there may be some overlap, each group will require different things from the company in order to become a satisfied customer. For example: readers want a lively, entertaining and informative newspaper, whereas advertisers want increased profile for their organisations and more customers. Councils may wish to inform and educate the local population; shareholders require a profitable newspaper; suppliers seek a healthy relationship with their customer and to be paid on time; and the staff want to work for a successful and interesting company.

You may be surprised that I have included both suppliers and staff on the above list. Although strictly speaking neither are customers, each group, however, forms an impression of the organisation and that impression is communicated to the outside world. If suppliers say it is difficult to get paid by the organisation for the services or products they have supplied, this may well spread a rumour that the organisation is in financial difficulty, or that they are awkward to deal with. This message can have a negative impact in the market place.

Likewise if the staff say negative things about the organisation they work for then word is likely to get around. Not only will the organisation find it difficult to recruit highly motivated and good quality staff but they will also find that this negative message spreads to their customer base, and therefore affects the organisation's reputation.

TOP TIPS

Remember that suppliers and staff are potential customers too, and they have a part to play in communicating your reputation, whether good or bad, to your market place.

ACTION POINT

Who are your customers? Make a list of them.

Now let's return to our newspaper example. One of the groups on that list was 'Readers', but readers can cover a vast number of different groups of people. There could be older readers, as well as younger ones who are single, and those with children, and of course both male and female readers. What is the lifestyle of the readers and their socio-economic background? What are their interests and those of the local community? What are their concerns?

Understanding who their readers are will enable the newspaper to tailor its news to appeal to that readership, and to produce the right style of newspaper with the right editorial content and therefore satisfy its customers. If it satisfies its customers by giving them the kind of newspaper they are interested in buying and reading, and by producing it on time and to an acceptable standard, then it will attract more readers, increase sales, attract more advertisers, recruit more staff because it is more successful and please its shareholders. Let's examine another example.

EXAMPLE

A legal firm will have a variety of customers (or clients) depending on the services it provides.

It will have ***business*** *clients, which can range from the small, one person firm to the large corporation. It could have clients who operate in the retail sector or in engineering, or construction, the professions and the not-for-profit sector. It will also have* ***consumers*** *(members of the public), who could be young people buying a property who need the conveyance service or those who require their estates to be managed and their Wills and Trusts to be drawn up. It could also have clients who are seeking a divorce, or require other legal advice such as litigation or criminal law.In addition, the legal firm could be acting on behalf of* ***overseas*** *clients in all kinds of business and personal legal matters.*

All these clients expect a certain standard of service from the legal firm, which if not received will result in them taking their business elsewhere.

Each client is also an individual and will therefore need to be treated as such. This means that some will demand a higher level of service than others. Some will have needs that are quite straightforward, others more complex requiring more time and 'hands on' assistance.

Some clients will have 'open' and 'friendly' personalities and will want to build close relationships with their legal advisers. Others will be quieter and more serious and want more of a formal approach, whilst others will be extremely demanding. So it is not merely enough to lump all your customers under the one heading of 'customers' but to examine what you are providing to each of them, to determine the level of service they require and to deliver it in a manner to make them feel they are getting exceptional customer service rather then merely adequate or good service.

In a service organisation 90% of staff have direct contact with the client compared to 10% in manufacturing.

Giving exceptional customer service is about understanding what different groups of customers require from you and what different individuals also require, then delivering that to meet or exceed their needs.

ACTION POINT

Return to your list of customers you drew up earlier.

Can you can break this down even further?

For example, can you divide it into groups of customers by type and size of business, into different sectors, or by age, life-style, gender or geographical area?

Can you add any more groups to your list of customers?

Have you added staff, suppliers and other groups on your list?

WHAT DO YOUR CUSTOMERS WANT?

When people buy a product or service they also consider the emotional factors that surround that purchase. Satisfying these emotional factors is what will help you to deliver good customer service.

Let's see what our groups of customers want from our newspaper example: and place after first paragraph.

Readers	Advertisers	Staff
The readers want: • Information • Entertainment • A relationship with the newspaper • Quality • Accuracy • Reputation • Content that reflects their interests • To be educated • Value for money • Continuity • Professionalism • Empathy	The advertisers want: • Customers • Job applicants • A relationship with the newspaper and its staff • Quality • Accuracy • Reputation • Brand • Value for money • Security/reliability • Results • Continuity • Professionalism • Empathy • Service	The staff want: • Job satisfaction • Enjoyment • A career • A salary package • Security • Relationships • Good feedback • Praise • Constructive criticism • Recognition • Professionalism • Training/ development • Pride • Commitment • Effective management • A positive company image • Responsibility • Purpose • Leadership • Communication • Loyalty

For example, when a woman pays for a hair cut, it is not just the quality of the cut and the style, but she will also take into consideration the attitude of the hairstylist and other staff; whether she is welcomed and feels comfortable, and the reputation of that salon.

In a restaurant you are considering not only the quality and quantity of food but also the atmosphere of the restaurant, its décor, the other clientele, the cleanliness and facilities of the restaurant, its location and accessibility.

And to cap it all, different members of staff will want varying degrees of the above. Your task as a manager (or owner/director) is to find out what motivates that particular staff member and then deliver it. In much the same way as we examined earlier, the good staff member finds out what the individual customer wants and delivers it.

By understanding and delivering these emotional factors to your customers, and satisfying them consistently, you will excel in providing customer service and gain a competitive advantage.

ACTION POINT

Take a look at *your* customer list and put the emotional factors beside each group of customers.

Then ask yourself if your organisation is delivering this.

WHY DO YOUR CUSTOMERS BUY?

Having looked at **what** customers expect when they buy, let's now examine **why** they buy.

People generally buy for two reasons:

- Objective reasons
- Subjective reasons

In order to deliver good customer service you will need to satisfy both of these.

Objective reasons

These are often associated with a physiological need. For example, you might buy a meal in a restaurant or café to satisfy a basic physiological need in that you are hungry. You dive into the first café you come to, or the only restaurant that has vacant spaces. A need to satisfy your hunger pang is the objective reason for buying.

In another example you might require the services of a solicitor, perhaps for a divorce, or to draw up a contract. You need to comply with the law. That is the objective reason for buying. So what are the subjective reasons?

Subjective reasons

Although you are hungry you might still ask yourself a series of questions before diving into the nearest café. For example: does it look like my sort of place? Who are the clientele and will I feel comfortable with them? Is the café clean? Does the restaurant have the right choice of food and beverages for me?

These are the subjective reasons. They are based on your personal preferences and are referred to as the psychological reasons involved in making a buying decision. Often, as we discussed previously, they are the emotional factors surrounding a purchase.

In respect of our legal firm example, you might be asking yourself the following questions before choosing a particular lawyer or legal firm:

- Does the lawyer understand my situation?
- Does the lawyer have the technical expertise to deal with my problem?
- Does he/she talk my language?
- Does the law firm provide an efficient service?

- What is its reputation?
- How am I treated when I telephone or visit them?
- How responsive are they to my requests and demands?
- Do they have the depth of specialist knowledge my situation requires?
- What is the cost and can I afford it?
- Can I relate to my lawyer?

The legal firm must make sure it delivers on all the above. If it fails to live up to expectations then the customer (or client) will be dissatisfied with the service, and might also tell others, thereby damaging future business for the firm.

If you are uncertain about the breakdown of your customers or about what, when and how they buy then Customer Relationship Management (CRM) software could help you. It analyses the buying habits and needs of your customers.

CUSTOMER RELATIONSHIP MANAGEMENT

Customer Relationship Management (CRM) software is a tool that can help you gain an insight into the behaviour of your customers. It contains a database that holds information on the buying habits of your customers, ie what they buy, when they buy, how often they purchase goods or services, and other relevant sales information. It is a technical solution, however, and not the ultimate solution to providing good customer relations. It is people who deliver good customer relations not computers.

However, CRM can help you to understand your customers and thereby become more responsive to their needs.

CRM can help you:

- Find out about your customers' purchasing habits, opinions and preferences
- Profile individuals and groups to market to them more effectively and therefore increase sales

- Change the way you operate to improve customer service and marketing

Using the analysis provided by CRM software you will then need to adapt your business to suit the needs of your customers.

There are many different types of software solutions available. You can purchase web based – and off-the shelf CRM solutions. Several software companies offer CRM applications that integrate with existing software. Alternatively you might wish for a tailored, bespoke solution, which will obviously be the most expensive. CRM consultants and software engineers can customise or create a CRM system and integrate it with your existing software.

CRM will help you capture the information you need to identify who your customers are and categorise their behaviour.

However, it will not be the right solution for every business and you should only examine this if you feel it will work for you. You might be able to get this information from conducting customer surveys (see chapter 9) or by analysing your existing database, or by analysing buying patterns of your website visitors.

CAPTURING INFORMATION ONLINE

If your business has a website and provides online customer service then you will already have information captured from when customers have entered their own details on the site when buying from you. This, and any other information, should be stored in a centralised customer database that will allow you to run all your systems from the same source, ensuring that everyone uses up-to-date information. Make sure that you can expand your systems if necessary. Carefully consider what data is collected and stored to ensure that only useful data is kept. Ensure that you comply with the data protection laws of your country, which state what information can be stored, and under which circumstances.

Using Customer Relationship Management software can help you to identify buying patterns, profile customers and develop sales strategies. With this information you can gain a better understanding of your customers' needs and then design a suitable reward programme, and target your most valuable customers with the right sales offerings. You can also identify those customers who are always complaining or causing trouble, taking up a disproportionate amount of staff time. If their problems can be identified and resolved quickly, your staff will have more time for other customers.

In order to be successful though you will need commitment from within the organisation, which brings us back once again to the 'people' element. All the relevant people in your organisation must know what information you need, why you need it, and how to use it.

QUICK RECAP

- *Different groups of customers have different needs, and individuals within the groups will also have different requirements.*
- *The more you know about your customers the more successful you will be in delivering to them the kind of exceptional service/products they require.*
- *Suppliers and staff form an impression of the organisation and that impression is communicated to the outside world – make sure it isn't a negative one.*
- *When people buy a product or service they also consider the emotional factors that surround that purchase.*
- *By understanding and delivering these emotional factors to your customers, and satisfying them consistently, you will excel in providing customer service and gain a competitive advantage.*
- *People generally buy for two reasons: objective and subjective and in order to deliver good customer service you will need to satisfy both of these.*
- *Customer Relationship Management Software can help you capture the information you need to identify who your customers are and categorise their behaviour.*
- *You might also be able to get this information from conducting customer surveys or by analysing your existing database, or by analysing the buying patterns of your website visitors.*

CHAPTER 3

Your customer service philosophy

With people being the key to delivering good customer service, management must make it clear to individuals what is expected of them. To do this you need to develop a customer service philosophy that runs right throughout your organisation. This chapter and the following chapters examine the eight steps you need to take in order to do this.

DEVELOPING A CUSTOMER SERVICE PHILOSOPHY

Developing a successful customer care philosophy can be broken down into eight key steps.

1. Develop a customer service orientated mission statement
2. Set standards of what is expected of everyone
3. Develop and adopt effective communications
4. Motivate staff for exceptional customer service
5. Provide ongoing staff training and development
6. Develop and incorporate a system to measure, monitor and reward performance
7. Plan for providing continuing customer care
8. And finally and most importantly involve your staff in all the above, foster good team working and lead by example.

Developing a customer service orientated mission statement

TOP TIPS

Staff can't deliver good customer service unless they know what the organisation stands for.

You need to define your organisation's personality and its mission. But this is not something you can do alone or delegate to management. In order for staff to value the organisation's mission to its customers and to deliver it, they must have ownership of it, which means everyone has a part to play in defining it.

You can do this by asking your staff how they view their organisation.

ACTION POINT

Get your staff together or into small groups if you have a number of staff. With a flip chart or white board ask them to come up with a series of words that they feel represents the organisation. For example: friendly, caring, go-ahead etc. Don't censor any words or rule them out, simply put them on the board for everyone to see.

EXAMPLE

A consulting engineering company was experiencing a number of difficulties internally. Staff seemed to be demotivated and client calls were not being returned promptly. A couple of client jobs had gone wrong, and in a difficult market where clients were hard fought for and won, the managing director decided they had to improve their internal marketing and customer care policy. An outside consultant was called in to find out what the staff's views were on the organisation. In a few sessions, with all staff participating, they came up with the following words that described their organisation:

- *Professional*
- *Progressive*
- *Friendly*
- *Trustworthy*
- *High quality*
- *Enthusiastic*
- *Approachable*
- *Efficient*

These are fine words, but do they go far enough? They could apply to any organisation.

So the next step is to personalise these words to define your organisation more specifically.

Taking the above example:

'XYZ Consulting Engineers is a friendly, professional and progressive company delivering high-quality work in a timely and efficient manner.'

So now we have a 'mission statement' and one that all the staff has contributed to. But how can we make this more easily identifiable for everyone to remember? The answer is by condensing it:

'XYZ Consulting Engineers delivers professionalism, consistently.'

ACTION POINT

Now take the words your staff have come up with and put it into a statement. This is essentially your mission statement. See if you (and your staff) can condense it and if so that it still makes sense. Is it simple enough for everyone in the organisation to remember?

So far so good. Now comes the tricky bit. Having defined it, you and everyone in your organisation must live up to it otherwise your customers will be disappointed.

TOP TIPS

Ensure that your staff believe in the mission statement and that they, and you, are committed to delivering it.

So let's go another step further.

ACTION POINT

Taking each word your staff have come up with ask them to rate their performance as a company on whether or not they are delivering it.

For example: On a scale of 0-5 where 5 is excellent and 0 is poor how well do you think XYZ is delivering what it promises?

- ❑ Professional
- ❑ Progressive
- ❑ Friendly
- ❑ Trustworthy
- ❑ High quality
- ❑ Enthusiastic
- ❑ Approachable
- ❑ Efficient

Now discuss with the staff the similarity or difference in the scores. How similar are they? How high or low are they?

Put this on hold for a moment before drawing any conclusions. Next you need to examine more specifically other areas of the organisation and how well or otherwise you are performing in respect of delivering good customer service. For example, if one of the words you have come up with is 'accessible' you need to measure just how well you score on the accessible rating. If one of your key words is 'friendly', how do you measure up to this word? How do your customers view your organisation?

First impressions

> You never get a second chance to make a first impression and neither does your organisation.

First impressions are often lasting impressions and could lose you vital business if they are negative ones. How many times have you walked out of a restaurant or hotel because you didn't like the look of the place? How many times have you telephoned an organisation to make an enquiry, to place an order, or make a booking and changed your mind because you were kept hanging on the telephone, or were passed from person to person, or found the member of staff on the other end of the line off-hand and unhelpful? Exactly! I hope it doesn't happen in your organisation, but you'd better check, just in case…

It is very easy to get blasé about your own organisation; after all, you work there, and therefore see it day in and day out, and because of this you eventually stop seeing it. It becomes wallpaper. You are too busy worrying about that next order, or that report, or what your boss thinks about you, or your personal problems to notice your surroundings. You don't see that things aren't how they should be. It often takes an outsider to point out the blindingly obvious.

So step back and take a good, long, hard look at your organisation from the prospective customer's point of view. Here is a questionnaire to help you. It can be adapted depending on your type of organisation.

How do you rate?

Assess your organisation – Is it giving out the correct impression?

Rate your organisation on a scale of 0-5 (5 = high, 0 = low) on the following criteria.

Location of the business

- ❑ Are you easily accessible to your customers and suppliers? (Do you need to be?)
- ❑ Can your customers find your offices, branch/outlet if they look you up on the internet?
- ❑ Is there a map giving directions?
- ❑ Are the telephone numbers and contact details easy to find?
- ❑ Is there car parking for visitors? Is this clearly displayed?
- ❑ Is the entrance clearly marked?
- ❑ Is the signage clear and creating the right image for your organisation?

Building outside

- ❑ Is it clean and well kept?
- ❑ Does it reflect the message you are giving to your customers? (Think about those keys words you've identified as describing your organisation – does the building meet this?)

Building inside

- ❑ Is the reception area clean, fresh and tidy?
- ❑ Are the public areas clean and tidy?
- ❑ Is the paintwork good?
- ❑ Is the furniture comfortable?
- ❑ Are there paintings on the walls? (What image do these communicate to the customer? Modern and go-ahead? Or perhaps traditional and comforting? It depends on your key words and how you with the organisation to be seen). Is this the image you want?
- ❑ Is the company sign clearly displayed?

- ❑ Are there magazines or company brochures available for your customers to read? (Are they up-to-date or will your customers be flicking through the pages of magazines that are a year or two old? If so you can hardly call yourself a go-ahead company, can you?)
- ❑ Have you used the reception or waiting areas space to promote your products/services?
- ❑ Are the interview or meeting rooms clean, tidy and comfortable?
- ❑ What kind of image do you want to give out in your conference or boardroom? Is this being achieved?
- ❑ Are the visitor toilets clean and well-equipped?

ACTION POINT

Now ask:

How did your organisation score?

How far away or close are you to living up to the key words you've already come up with? Have you identified areas that need improving?

Make a list of these and say how you wish to improve them.

You'll also need to draw up a timetable and budget.

Take care of the minor points first. For example, you might not be able to afford to refurbish the reception area of your building but you could make a plan to do this in two or three years' time. Meanwhile, there could be some very low cost actions you can take, like refreshing the area by painting it, putting up new pictures or making sure there are fresh flowers in reception. The least you can do is to ensure that the public areas are tidied and cleaned on a daily basis.

Taking care of the physical aspects is important – take time to make sure they're right.

How your staff create the right impression

Now let's look more closely at how the staff communicate the correct impression, ie the one you desire.

How do you rate?

Assess your organisation. Is it giving out the correct impression?

Rate your organisational staff on a scale of 0-5 (5 = high, 0 = low) on the following criteria.

Reception and front line staff

- ❑ The receptionist – is he/she smartly dressed or in uniform provided?
- ❑ Is he/she clean and presentable?
- ❑ Does he/she smile on greeting the customer?
- ❑ Does the receptionist get the customer's name and use it?
- ❑ Does the receptionist invite the customer to take a seat?
- ❑ Does he/she offer the customer a coffee or tea? (If appropriate).
- ❑ If there is a delay does the receptionist keep the customer informed?

The receptionist is often the first person in an organisation to come into contact with the customer. It is vitally important, therefore, that you have the right person for this job. This also applies to all those employees who are front line staff. But all too often companies put 'the dragon' on reception and some organisations seem to recruit and place in the front line the most unhelpful individuals they can find. Is it because nobody else wants to work with them? Or is it because you have recruited in a hurry, or because you are not very good at interviewing and appointing staff? Taking time to get this right could save you a great deal of time in the future not to mention money.

Also ensure that your reception and public areas do not become gossip zones. I have overheard staff grumbling about their company and the individuals within the company on many occasions. It is highly unprofessional and creates a very negative opinion in the mind of the customer.

Answering the telephone

The telephone may be the first point of contact for the customer within your organisation. Indeed in some cases it may be the only point of contact. So how do you rate on a good telephone answering manner?

How is the telephone answered?

- ❑ Do you have a policy that it is answered within five rings, or do all your staff leave their telephones on voice mail and **never** return calls? Is this appropriate behaviour for an organisation that promotes itself as being customer friendly? I don't think so!
- ❑ How often do your customers get passed around between departments?
- ❑ If you have an automated call system is it helpful and appropriate? Most people hate them, but sadly they are a fact of life. Is it important to your organisation for the customer to speak to a real person rather than press buttons and feed information into a telephone keypad? If you are providing a product or service to an elderly group of customers then personal contact will be extremely important to them, and the pressing of buttons in an automated call system highly inappropriate.

Staff behaviour and attitude

- ❑ When your staff speak to the customer what is their manner like? Those who are abrupt, impatient and can only speak in monosyllables are not what you need. Neither are individuals who chatter away endlessly. If you have staff who are handling complaints then they need to know how to do this professionally (see chapter 16 for more on this).

- ❑ How do your staff behave towards your customers?
- ❑ How should they address them – by their surname or first name?
- ❑ How should the staff respond to customer enquiries?
- ❑ What is the length of time they should respond to enquiries by telephone or letter?
- ❑ Do you have a policy to state this and if so is it monitored regularly to see if it is being delivered?

ACTION POINT

Now ask:

How did your staff score?

How far away or close are you to living up to the key words you've already come up with? Have you identified areas that need improving?

Make a list of these and say how you wish to improve them.

THE WORKPLACE ENVIRONMENT

In chapter 2 we looked at what various groups of customers demand from an organisation, and one of these groups was staff. If an organisation doesn't care for its staff then the staff are hardly likely to care for the customers. So not only does the workplace environment need to be the right one for the customers it also needs to be right for the staff.

How do you rate?

Here is another questionnaire for you to asses how the work environment scores with the staff. We will examine other issues important to staff in the following chapters. Again score 5 = high and 0 = poor.

Staff areas

- ❑ Work stations – are these comfortable, functional and adequate for the task?
- ❑ Rest room/canteen – is there somewhere for the staff to relax when off duty, or to eat their lunch? Is this clean, tidy and well equipped?
- ❑ Toilets – are there adequate toilet facilities? Are they cleaned regularly?
- ❑ Equipment – do staff have the right equipment for the job? Inadequate and frequently failing equipment is often a demotivating factor and causes unnecessary delays and therefore lost profits.

Are there any areas that you need to look at and correct? You might also like to ask your customers, suppliers and other visitors for their views and requirements. These might differ from your view because sometimes it is hard to be objective; being objective is paramount if you wish to project the right image to your customers.

ACTION POINT

1. Write out your full mission statement
2. Write out your condensed mission statement
3. Toilets- are there adequate clean toilet facilities?
4. Draw up a timetable of when you can improve these elements.
5. Put beside this who is responsible for doing what.

You might need to return to this after working through the rest of this book, particularly if you have staff and management training issues to address.

MAKE SURE THE MESSAGES DON'T GET MIXED

Organisations often spend vast amounts of money in getting their external message right and fail to do the same inside the company. If you are telling your customers that you are a progressive organisation, approachable, professional and reliable and yet when customers approach you they get a sloppy service, the premises are shabby and nobody ever returns their calls, then the customer will be gravely disappointed and will take their business elsewhere.

Be consistent

In order to deliver excellent customer service your message has to be consistent both inside and outside the organisation. It is not merely a cosmetic exercise, though sadly many organisations think it is. You have to live the message.

Building a reputation

Building a reputation for excellence takes a considerable amount of time, destroying it can take seconds. By constantly checking the above factors you can begin to build a clearly defined image and reputation for your organisation.

QUICK RECAP

- *Having a clearly defined image of what your organisation stands for, consistently communicating it and living up to that image is what it takes to stand out from the crowd.*
- *Staff need to be involved in developing this image and in writing a customer service orientated mission statement to sum this up.*
- *You never get a second chance to make a first impression and neither does your organisation.*
- *First impressions are often lasting impressions and could lose you vital business if they are negative..*
- *Take a long, hard look at your organisation from the prospective customer's viewpoint: is it giving out the right impression?*
- *Are the staff giving out the right impression?*
- *Ask your customers, staff and other visitors for their views.*
- *Make sure your front line staff are fully trained and able and willing to deal with the customer effectively and efficiently.*
- *Ensure you have a policy that says how the telephone should be answered and how calls should be handled.*
- *Ensure you have a policy that states how customer complaints should be handled.*
- *If an organisation doesn't care for the workplace environment and the well-being of its staff, then the staff won't care for the organisation.*
- *Be consistent in your messages both inside and outside the organisation.*

CHAPTER 4

Setting standards

In order to provide excellent customer service your staff need to know what is expected of them. Developing and agreeing a clear mission statement is the first step in this process. The next is having a set of standards which staff and management can follow. This chapter examines the different types of standards you might wish to consider and how you can successfully draw them up and implement them.

DEVELOPING A SET OF STANDARDS

In order to prevent misunderstandings between staff and management, and between individuals it is always a good idea to develop a set of standards which set out how you expect staff to behave towards customers. Standards can also encompass how you wish the services you provide to customers to be delivered, or can set the acceptable level of quality that the products you manufacture should meet. You might also have environmental standards, which set out a clear policy on matters such as recycling and purchasing.

Listed below are the more common standards. You can decide which ones you adopt dependent on your business.

Common standards

- Behaviour
- Dress/appearance
- Delivery of your service or key performance standards
- Quality of your product
- Environmental
- Customer complaints handling

Dress and behaviour standards

> Setting dress and behaviour codes can be highly contentious areas.

In order to avoid dissent you need to involve your staff in drawing up these standards. This gives them ownership, which means they will be happier in complying with the rules once set. If you have a large organisation it will be difficult to involve everyone in this process, so setting up a small committee or team, with a representative from each department may be the answer. This representative will take responsibility for obtaining feedback from team members, and reporting back any developments and outcomes.

Once the policy is made and implemented ensure that this is communicated to all staff and that new members of staff are fully inducted. This will result in fewer mistakes. If you need to tell a member of staff that their dress or manner of behaviour is not acceptable then you will have the written standards to back you up, and evidence that they were told this during their induction.

Behaviour standard

Some organisations see no need to have a dress code. This is often dependent on the type of business and the customers that the business serves. Having a behaviour standard or code may be a very different matter. For example, you may wish to state that all telephone calls are to be answered within three to five rings and that the caller announces his name and department on answering, or that all customers are addressed formally by their surname.

The behaviour code can also include items such as the time by which staff should be at their desks or on the shop floor. It can include behaviour around smoking breaks, ie how many are premissable and where staff take these breaks. In some companies staff are not permitted to linger around the work premises but can only smoke inside their cars in the car park, or indeed away from the car park and completely off the company premises.

It can cover the number and timing of refreshment breaks, or security issues such as ensuring staff areas are kept secure and making sure that all visitors are signed in and out again and issued a pass while they are on the premises. Other aspects of a behaviour code can include: use of emails and internet browsing during work hours; not drinking alcohol during work hours even when entertaining clients; cleanliness and tidiness of work stations; a clear desk policy at the end of the working day, plus more. It is very much up to you as the owner or director of the business what you feel appropriate to include in any behaviour code or standard, but if you are drawing up a new code of staff behaviour where none has previously existed it wouldn't do any harm to involve your staff in this.

The more involvement your staff have in drawing up a code, the greater their commitment to making it work.

HANDLING CUSTOMER COMPLAINTS

It is advisable for you to draw up standards of how you expect your staff to handle customer complaints and provide training for them to confidently deliver this. A code or standard of how customer complaints should be dealt with will not only help the individual but it will also enable you to measure that member of staff's performance against the standard.

TOP TIPS

Regularly review standards, and update and amend if necessary

Measure and monitor performance against the standard

Reward those staff who consistently deliver or exceed it.

PERFORMANCE STANDARDS

In order to deliver exceptional customer service you should also agree clear objectives with each member of staff for their performance. These objectives will fit with the organisation's overall objectives, therefore ensuring that each employee is aware how their contribution helps towards the organisation's goals.

The individual's performance can then be measured against these agreed standards at regular performance appraisals. (See chapter 8 for more on this).

Before setting an individual's performance standards you need to make sure that these are realistic in terms of the task they perform within your organisation. Each process or procedure that is carried out by that staff member, or that team, needs to be examined to ensure that it matches the customer's experience of your organisation, and the customer's satisfaction with your products or service.

To do this you need to:

- Examine in detail how the service is delivered
- Evaluate the critical success points in the process
- Define service standards and objectives for these essential points
- Establish service delivery procedures to ensure they meet your customer's satisfaction
- Create and set the standard for the level of service delivery within the organisation

Key drivers

One of the ways you can examine these procedures and processes is to analyse and identify the key stages in each service provided that meets the customer's satisfaction levels.

EXAMPLE

Plumbwater sells a range of plumbing equipment supplies to the trade. They operate a call handling centre with 10 telemarketing personnel handling incoming calls from individuals placing orders (inbound), and outgoing calls to new and lapsed customers (outbound) to try and win new orders.

The call operators are also responsible for trying to cross sell and up-sell other products to existing customers and to inform them of special offers.

Each operator has a set of objectives which includes targets for new orders won and how many calls they should handle in a month. These objectives and targets are set to meet the overall organisation's objectives. In addition to meeting these targets, Plumbwater prides itself on delivering a high level of customer satisfaction. With this in mind the company has standards set for each operator against which their performance is also measured in terms of providing customer satisfaction, and not just meeting sales targets.

This is fine because each operator knows and understands what is expected of him both from the sales objectives he needs to meet and the performance level criteria to provide customer satisfaction. However, if a manager then decides to push his staff harder to increase outbound calls and win a higher number of new orders, ie increase the sales objectives, this could result in:

- *The staff having less time trying to help existing customers*
- *The staff not getting so much information from new customers which in turn means a lack of marketing information that could be used to create more successful marketing campaigns*
- *Eventual decrease in sales because marketing is poorly targeted and communicated*
- *Less time for the staff member to cross sell to existing customers*
- *A decline in the quality of service to existing customers*
- *A decrease in the satisfaction level of customers*
- *Lower sales*

Conducting a customer satisfaction survey could help in this example to determine the number of outbound calls an operator could make without impinging on the delivery of the expected level of customer satisfaction.

For example Plumbwater could measure:

- Operator technical knowledge
- Operator courtesy and friendliness
- Speed with which the call was answered
- Number of calls required to get a problem solved
- Operator's communication skills
- Operator's patience

By then conducting an analysis of the customer's answers, and examining their satisfaction level, the company can derive which factors have the greatest impact on the customer's perceived level of satisfaction. It can examine what is needed to improve service levels, and what to keep at the same level. For example, if operator product knowledge is lacking, Plumbwater could implement some training. However, if speed with which the calls are answered is important the company might need to look at the number of operators they have and ask whether it is enough. They might need to draft in temporary help, or perhaps reorganise the work load and re-examine sales objectives, and/or restructure the team to get greater efficiency.

ACTION POINT

Examine the sales targets you have set and the objectives for each member of staff: are they realistic?

Is customer service being sacrificed because of unrealistic goals?

Get each member of staff to write down what they see as the key areas of their job, or if they have a job description, to review it and rank each task in order of importance in meeting customer satisfaction. Then conduct a customer survey to see if the two marry up.

Examine what you need to do, if anything, to improve customer satisfaction. Do you need to restructure an individual's job, or restructure a team or department? Do you need to introduce new technology, recruit more staff or set new sales targets or objectives?

Things change – markets, customers' needs and wants, products and services, technology. When was the last time you examined what you were delivering and how? It is very easy to carry on doing what you have always done without realising until too late that the market has changed and you and your organisation haven't.

Encourage your staff to contribute new ideas and suggest better ways of doing things. After all, if they're in the front line and interfacing with customers, they hear all the customer's views, gripes and complaints.

TOP TIPS

Involve your staff in setting standards

Ask your customers what is important to them (see chapter 9 for more on this)

Adhere to those standards yourself

THE STAFF HANDBOOK

The staff handbook can be a valuable tool in ensuring your staff are aware of the organisation's policies, mission and standards. Here are some guidelines on what the staff handbook might contain.

Introduction
- About the organisation
- Its structure and background
- Its mission statement

1. Conduct and discipline
- Expected conduct
- Behaviour, dress and other codes as required
- Confidentiality
- Disciplinary procedures
- Grievance procedures

2. Salaries and benefits
- Salaries
- Pension schemes
- Permanent health insurance
- Private medical insurance
- Public and Bank Holiday entitlement

3. Administrative procedures and rules
- Standard working hours and timekeeping
- Flexible working hours
- Holiday rules
- Sickness rules
- Maternity policy
- Compassionate leave
- Allowances and expenses

- Driving on firm's business
- Eye testing for those using computer monitors

4. Personnel policies and procedures

- Induction
- Training procedures
- Staff appraisal procedures
- Recruitment procedures
- Statement of policy in accordance with the health & safety laws
- Policy on harassment
- Equal opportunities policy

5. Client services policy

- Clients' complaints procedures
- Telephone answering policy

QUICK RECAP

- *In order to prevent misunderstandings between staff and management, and between individuals, develop a set of standards on how you expect staff to behave towards customers.*
- *Standards can also encompass how you wish the services you provide to customers to be delivered, or the acceptable level of quality of the products you manufacture. The more common standards are:*
  - *Behaviour*
  - *Dress/appearance*
  - *Delivery of your service*
  - *Quality of your product*
  - *Environmental*
  - *Customer complaints*
- *In order to avoid dissent you need to involve your staff in drawing up these standards.*
- *Make it clear to staff what is expected of them and give them a real sense of personal responsibility.*
- *Each process or procedure that is carried out needs to be examined to ensure that it matches the customer's experience of your organisation, and the customer's satisfaction with your products or service.*
- *Examine what you need to do, if anything, to improve customer satisfaction.*
- *Adhere to those standards yourself and encourage your staff to contribute new ideas/better ways of doing things.*

CHAPTER 5

Improving communication

Most problems within organisations boil down to two things: weak management and poor communication. Both lead to disaffected staff, which leads to poor customer service. Communication is not just a case of slapping out a newsletter or bulletin, or holding meetings, but involves actively inviting opinions, talking to individuals face-to-face, and listening to them. Yes, it takes time, but it is essential to help your organisation deliver that excellence in customer service. This chapter examines how you can improve communication in your organisation and therefore improve motivation.

THE BENEFITS OF IMPROVED COMMUNICATION

You need to create an organisation where instructions can be given and carried out effectively and efficiently.

There are many benefits to be gained from improving communication. Here are just a few:

- Greater awareness
- Greater efficiency
- Information given to staff helps them to perform well and to deliver better service
- Staff are more motivated if they feel part of a team
- More focused staff
- The organisation is more efficient in the eyes of the client
- Greater dependability
- Satisfied clients
- Better profitability
- Fewer conflicts within the firm therefore less time wasted on fire fighting and crisis handling

Communicating effectively should be the simplest thing in the world, we talk and listen; I tell you want to do and you do it. Right? No, wrong. Mistakes are made because communication, or rather the lack of it or misinterpretation, is often at the heart of the problem.

You cannot be an effective manager unless you know how to communicate confidently in any circumstance; this can be on a one-to-one basis, with your team, with the customers, or indeed, if you are senior management or a director, to the entire organisation. But with more and more transactions being conducted by email and text, we are in danger of losing the art of communicating effectively. It now appears that people at all levels would rather use email than pick up a telephone, even if the person they wish to communicate with is sitting at the next desk!

Some organisations are designed to deal with customers only by email and through their web sites. Amazon is one such company. This is fine to a degree, just as long as customers have the equipment and ability to purchase online, but it will alienate certain sectors of society who cannot use modern technology or who don't have access to it. This might be acceptable to the company. In this case an organisation needs to have in place excellent systems and knowledgeable, efficient staff, because when problems occur, as they will, it can be extremely frustrating for the customer dealing with an anonymous person at the end of an email.

EXAMPLE

An accountancy firm was finding that an increasing number of clients were leaving to go to a rival firm. The directors were very concerned about this and couldn't understand why. They told the staff that they would have to buck their ideas up and provide better client service but nothing changed. Clients were still leaving and what's more highly qualified and motivated staff were also leaving. The firm called in an outside consultant to help them find out what was going wrong. The consultant discovered the following problems:

- *A lack of communication from the top down which meant that the staff were making assumptions about what was happening in the business. These were incorrect and the rumours were becoming destructive.*
- *There was a lack of communication between the various people who worked on the client's accounts. This meant that work was being duplicated (a waste of money and time) and that the client was receiving two, sometimes three telephone calls from different people about the same thing, which was annoying for the client.*
- *There was also a lack of communication from the bottom up. Staff felt the directors were unapproachable and therefore were reluctant to inform them if there was a problem, leaving the client to discover it.*

*In the above example the directors needed to accept that no matter how busy they were they **had** to make time to communicate on a regular basis with the staff and to put into place some formal means of communication.*

ACTION POINT

How good are you at communicating? Try answering 'yes' or 'no' to the simple questionnaire below.

1. Do you praise your staff as readily as you criticise them?
2. Do you communicate equally often with all your staff, juniors as well as seniors?
3. Do you hold regular, planned meetings in addition to ad hoc emergency sessions?
4. Do your staff consistently tell you what you need to hear and not just what they think you would like to hear?
5. Do staff communicate effectively with each other?
6. Have you reviewed and reconsidered your communication needs and methods within the last 12 months?
7. Do all staff (including you) have an up-to-date job description?
8. Have you had formal training in leading group discussion?
9. Do you believe that you are aware of the problems of your staff?
11. Do all staff know how their work contributes to the work of the business as a whole?

Now get a member of your staff (or a few) to answer the questions as they see them about you. Compare the two. How realistic were you? Do you think you are a better communicator than you actually are?

Recognising poor communication

Have you ever heard comments like?

> 'Nobody told me.'
> 'I didn't know it was my job...'
> 'What are these forms for?'
> 'I assumed you'd know what I meant.'

If so then communication within your organisation needs to be improved. Remember communication is a two-way process.

Different methods of communication

Here is a list of some of the various means of communication within an organisation. Not all will be appropriate for your organisation:

- Email
- Letters
- Telephone
- Fax
- Memos
- Intranet
- Meetings
- Social events
- Staff newsletter
- Messages
- Training
- Appraisals
- Coaching
- Mentoring
- Briefings
- Brainstorming sessions
- Socialising within the workplace
- Rumours and gossip
- Post mortems/feedback sessions
- Induction
- Exit interviews
- Notice boards.

ACTION POINT

Review the list of the different methods of communications above and put a tick beside the ones that you are currently using, and then another tick against the ones you think might work within your organisation.

IMPROVING COMMUNICATION

Sometimes formal communication is too restrictive. Most communication is through gossip and rumour so it is occasionally better to feed the formal information into this informal network – it will get around a lot quicker!

Communication is not telling – it is involving. And it has to come from the bottom up as well as the top down. So in order to make it more effective you need to encourage contributions from your staff. How can you do this?

You could implement a staff suggestion scheme and give rewards for the ideas implemented. Remember it is also important to provide feedback on the ideas that were not implemented, giving genuine reasons as to why they are unworkable. Most companies are brimming with ideas and yet one of the many talents managers seem to have is destroying them. Make sure you have a system to capture ideas to explore and discuss them. Failure to do so leads to demoralisation and a feeling of 'Why should I bother' among employees.

TOP TIPS

By encouraging employees to put forward ideas and wherever possible allowing them to develop and implement those ideas you will not only motivate them but will give them a real sense of involvement and responsibility.

Here are a few suggestions on how to improve communication:

- Introduce regular newsletters/bulletins which could be in the form of an email, e-newsletter/bulletin or a printed version. You might like to ask for a volunteer to produce this. It doesn't have to be written by management, although managers will contribute to it. Alternatively, this might be a task that a member of staff could take on as a developmental role, or as part of their job function.
- Put announcements on notice boards where staff will see them, eg in the staff rest room or canteen, or by the photocopier.
- Walk around your workplace and get feedback first hand from staff and even customers.

- Build project teams to get staff to understand each other's roles and stimulate working together.
- Provide training and open discussion at training sessions with action points.
- Know your people as individuals and take time to talk to them.
- Give regular team briefings or cross departmental meetings/ briefings.

EXAMPLE

An equipment/exhibition sales and graphic display company implemented a monthly scheme whereby staff nominate and vote for a member of staff as 'Employee of the Month'. The staff member nominated is a person who has gone the extra mile for a customer, or who consistently delivers excellence in customer service. One such member of staff gave up his weekend to deliver graphic displays to a customer in Monaco, driving from the UK and back to do so to ensure that the customer had the graphics he needed on time for a critical exhibition. The 'Employee of the Month' is given gift vouchers and is recognised in the monthly staff newsletter, which is sent to all staff throughout the company's five branches. At the end of the year all staff vote on the 'Employees of the Month' and an overall 'Employee of the Year' is chosen and rewarded with a cheque, a plaque and a gift.

The above example not only illustrates a method of communication – a staff newsletter – but also encourages staff participation and involvement.

BENEFITS OF TEAM BRIEFINGS

Team briefings can help to improve communication within an organisation. They can reduce misunderstanding, increase co-operation when introducing change, improve staff commitment and reduce the damage resulting from rumours.

In team briefings you can:

- Inform of progress against budgets, sales achieved etc.
- Mention an individual's achievements, completion of a difficult task, passing exams etc.
- Give highly motivating public recognition to those members of staff who deserve it.
- Include such matters as changes to the holiday rotas, revised safety rules etc.

You should allow time for questions. Any grumbles must be heard, noted and acted upon.

ACTION POINT

Reviewing the list you made earlier regarding the communication methods you could introduce into your organisation, can you now add to this?

Beside each method put your ideas of who might be responsible for them, how and when they might be implemented. But before announcing them involve your staff – ask them what methods of communication they would like to see introduced and how they think they might work, also ask for their ideas of how they should be implemented and who might be responsible for what.

The following chapters on motivating, training and coaching are also concerned with improving communication within an organisation.

QUICK RECAP

- *Most problems within organisations boil down to two things: weak management and poor communication.*
- *Communication involves actively inviting opinions, talking to individuals face-to-face and listening to them.*
- *Staff need to feel they are simultaneously informed, involved and sharing in the success of the organisation.*
- *Encourage your staff to contribute new ideas and suggest better ways of doing things.*
- *The benefits to be gained from improving communication include better delivery of customer service, more focused staff and better profitability.*
- *Communication is not telling – it is involving. It has to come from the bottom up as well as the top down.*
- *Make sure you have a system to capture ideas and to explore and discuss them.*

CHAPTER 6

Motivating your staff

It is your staff who deliver the service and who sell the products. They are the main interface with the customers. Getting the right staff, and training and motivating them, is a vital part of providing exceptional customer service. But this doesn't just happen of its own accord. Good customer service demands good managers. This chapter examines the skills and qualities you need, and how to motivate your staff to give exceptional customer service.

MOTIVATING FOR EXCEPTIONAL CUSTOMER SERVICE

Good customer service starts at the TOP with good management.

Just as good parents lead by example, and enthusiastic and imaginative teachers inspire, so good managers and directors lead by setting the correct example to their staff and by inspiring and enthusing them.

Many managers feel they have to behave in an autocratic way and are unapproachable. This is guaranteed to alienate those who report to them. They feel the need to focus on the negative rather than the positive by going around and spotting what is wrong rather than what people are doing right. This is a sure-fire way to demotivate staff.

The good manager/director will have an acute awareness that people matter and an understanding of the many human characteristics which can inhibit progress. What will motivate one person might not motivate another. In order to understand what makes your staff tick you need to understand that people work for a variety of reasons. In addition, they all have different personalities and different levels of intellect. The good manager understands this and knows what and how to motivate each individual member of his team to give of their best.

Motivated staff deliver exceptional customer service.

In order to get the best out of your staff you will need persistence and patience accompanied by a willingness to adapt or alter direction when required. The effective manager/director will embrace change, have enthusiasm for the training and development of his staff, be prepared to face problems and deal with them, and know how obstacles can be overcome.

Disaffected staff will give poor customer service.

Some demotivating factors

There are a number of factors which can affect staff performance and therefore their motivation and attitude towards customers. We have already looked at some of these under the heading of the workplace environment, here are some further demotivating factors.

- Dirty offices
- Cramped working conditions
- Poor or too bright light
- Unreliable vending machines
- Photocopiers that persistently break down
- Unresolved conflict, eg who is responsible for filing, making the tea etc.
- Rules which are perceived as petty or pointless
- Adverse effect of work on home life
- Weak supervision
- Real or apparent favouritism
- Telephone system inefficient
- Computers always breaking down
- Bosses frequently disappearing without telling their staff when they will be back or where they are going

Correcting these alone will not in itself make staff motivated but it will at least restore them to a contented state. The good manager will always take time to see that these factors are as good as they ought to be, and are not a constant irritation which erodes enthusiasm.

The small things matter.

As people climb the management ladder they can often become isolated from the front line staff – shut behind their doors in their ivory towers. Of course, you might work very closely with your staff, or your organisation might be a small one, but if it isn't then here is a simple exercise you should do to find out exactly how things really are on the shop floor.

ACTION POINT

Walking the Job

1. Put a time in your diary to visit part of the organisation.
   Work out what you want to achieve from the visit beforehand.
   Make your presence known to the people in charge. It is usually best not to give warning to them because they will then prepare and give you a false impression of what life is really like for them. However, you must inform the managers or heads of department once you are there, as you do not wish to undermine their authority.
2. Make sure you are well briefed, ie names of key people, output, sales figures etc.
3. Don't turn the walkabout into a state visit, or it becomes an ego trip.
4. Walk around the workplace, talk and listen to as many people as possible. Start gently, some people may be nervous or overawed by you. Ask them what they do and get them to show you. Have some questions worked out in advance. Take the opportunity to praise. Don't make critical remarks or reprimand. Listen carefully. Thank the people you've met.
5. Have a look at general conditions, like the state of the toilets, cleanliness, lighting, heating etc.
6. Remember you are not on a fault finding expedition but genuinely trying to see how things really are.
7. Conclude by discussing your observations with the local managers and supervisors.
8. Finally, analyse whether it was a success. If you were met by friendly people who smiled and relaxed in your presence and talked to you frankly then you are showing signs of an effective leader and your organisation is far more likely to be customer friendly.

WHAT DOES MOTIVATION MEAN?

Motivation is encouraging, inspiring, influencing and stimulating people to perform well.

Motivation is making people feel they *want* to work, and making them feel good about what they are doing. The signs that show that individuals within an organisation are motivated are:

- Employees are happy in their work
- Employees co-operate rather than compete
- Employees take responsibility for their work
- There is a low level of absence from work
- Performance is high

The symptoms of poor motivation within an organisation are:

- Employees appearing unhappy and complaining about unimportant matters
- Employees refusing to co-operate and being obstructive
- Employees blaming others for their mistakes
- A high level of absence from work owing to illness
- Poor time-keeping
- Staying away from the workplace as long as possible by dragging out tea breaks etc.
- Output falling below set quality and quantity standards
- Jobs not being done on time

So what is the effect of poor motivation on an organisation?

- Dissatisfied customers
- A rise in the number of customer complaints
- Higher recruitment and staffing costs
- Lower profits
- Lower productivity
- Could ultimately lead to redundancies and even the company closing

TOP TIPS

Happy staff make happy customers = increased sales and profits

ACTION POINT

Examine your own organisation

What is the level of absenteeism? Have you seen this increase or decrease lately?

Is there a culture of blame in your organisation?

Are people late back from lunch or tea breaks?

Do they take too long to do simple tasks?

Are they constantly complaining?

If so then re-examine those workplace conditions mentioned earlier to see if some of these are causing disaffected staff.

You also need to look at the following reasons for demotivated staff.

MANAGERIAL ACTIONS THAT DEMOTIVATE STAFF

- Refusal to delegate
- Inconsistency
- Unable or unwilling to praise
- Lack of clear direction
- Not keeping staff informed
- Not consulting over key issues
- Being aggressive or bad tempered

MOTIVATING FACTORS

So what motivates staff to give of their best? People come to work for a variety of reasons, and understanding why individuals within your team or organisation come to work can be one of the first steps to finding out what motivates them.

People work because:

- They need money, and work to earn some.
- They enjoy the company of others and relating to people, they like the social side that work gives them.
- Some people need to be intellectually challenged and get bored if they are not.
- Some people enjoy a particular form of work and do it because they enjoy it.
- Some people work to compensate for other areas of their life. They may be unhappy and dominated at home. At work they may be able to exercise that power. They may want independence.
- Some people need a framework for their lives – work can provide this.
- Some people need praise and self-esteem. They need personal development.

TOP TIPS

The good motivating manager understands what makes the individual staff member tick.

People are generally motivated by the following:

- A sense of achievement
- Recognition
- Amount of responsibility

- Prospects of advancement
- Interesting work
- Growth possibilities

MOTIVATING STAFF FOR EXCEPTIONAL CUSTOMER SERVICE

In order to feel involved and motivated the staff need to have a sense of group pride, ie pride in their team and/or organisation. They need a shared sense of purpose, with good interaction between staff and between staff and managers, and a genuine desire to see the organisation succeed.

So they need:

- To know that what they are doing is worthwhile
- To be appreciated
- To have confidence in themselves and the value of the job
- To have confidence in the team/company
- Encouragement to use their own initiative
- Concern for their individual circumstances
- Positive and constructive feedback on what they have done or are doing
- Consultation over the work they will be doing in the future
- Clear objectives
- Openness and frankness
- Clear and effective decision making
- Regular and timely reviews

How can you do this?

Give the individual as much control over their work as you can. With them, examine their job and redesign it in any way to give them this control. Nobody likes a manager or supervisor breathing down their neck so allow them to get on with their work without checking up on them every five minutes. Along with this goes trust and the ability to delegate. Many people do not delegate because they consider they are the only people who can do the job, they are often insecure or afraid of losing control. This means staff become indifferent. They feel they are undervalued and not trusted. Delegating will boost productivity and enhance motivation.

> **TOP TIPS**
>
> **Successful delegation**
>
> Ask yourself:
>
> Is this person capable of doing the task I wish to delegate?
>
> Will they be able to do it without constant supervision?
>
> Will they check with me if they run into problems?
>
> If you can answer 'yes' then delegate. You will be providing a powerful motivator.

Allow individuals to make mistakes and give them the opportunity to say why they made the mistake and how they can avoid it or improve their performance in the future.

Make sure you give your staff clear direction and that they know and understand what is expected of them. The standards you have in place will provide excellent guidelines as to what you expect (discussed in chapter 4). These standards need to have been fully explained to them and understood.

Provide regular and constructive feedback. Give praise when due. Be fair and consistent. And remember communication, which we examined in the previous chapter, plays a considerable part in helping to motivate staff to perform well.

Giving constructive criticism

Praising people when they do something well will motivate them much more strongly than criticising them. And **constantly** criticising is guaranteed to demotivate. There are occasions, however when criticism needs to be given. This should always be**constructive**. So, how do you do this?

If you need to give criticism, check it is specific and not a personal attack. For example:

'Chris, I've noticed your sales figures have been low these last two months why is that?'

Not,

'Chris, you'd better pull your socks up and get some more sales otherwise it'll be curtains for you.'

Don't jump to conclusions; they might be the wrong ones. Chris's sales figures might be low because he has personal problems or because of ill health.

If handled in the correct way, people are often self critical. For example, if you need to tackle a member of staff over a customer complaint then asking the staff member **what** went wrong and **how** he can handle it more effectively in the future is better than balling him out.

Give the other person the chance to state his case and get all the facts. Then you can ask for suggestions to bring about the change you require. For example, 'What are your ideas for improving this?' or 'So, how should you deal with this in future?'

TOP TIPS

Boosting motivation

Deliberately shift your vocabulary from *my* company to *our* company

Be accessible. Always keep an open door policy and show you listen.

Make colleagues feel that they have the power to do things.

Take time to say 'good morning' and take a personal interest.

Aim for four pieces of praise to every one piece of constructive criticism.

Know yourself – get feedback. An honest, open relationship is key to successful staff motivation and hence exceptional customer service.

Your mood matters. It will make others feel good, or otherwise.

Take your job seriously but not yourself.

QUICK RECAP

- *Motivating your staff is a vital part of providing exceptional customer service.*
- *Good customer service demands good managers.*
- *The good manager/director will have an acute awareness that people matter and an understanding of the many human characteristics which can inhibit progress.*
- *To get the best out of your staff you will need persistence and patience accompanied by a willingness to adapt or alter direction when required.*
- *The effective manager/director will embrace change, have enthusiasm for the training and development of his staff, be prepared to face problems and deal with them, and know how obstacles can be overcome.*
- *Motivation is encouraging, inspiring, influencing, and stimulating people to perform well.*
- *Happy staff make happy customers which means increased sales and profits.*
- *People come to work for a variety of reasons, and understanding why individuals within your team or organisation come to work can be one of the first steps to finding out what motivates them.*
- *In order to feel involved and motivated the staff need to have a sense of group pride, ie pride in their team and/or organisation.*
- *Give the individual as much control over the work they do as you can, don't keep checking up on them.*
- *Make sure you give your staff clear direction and that they know and understand what is expected of them.*
- *Communication plays a considerable part in helping to motivate staff to perform well.*

CHAPTER 7

Training and development

In order to provide good customer service you need to have knowledgeable and confident staff. This means providing ongoing training for them. It is amazing how many organisations throw their staff in at the deep end with little or no training and just expect them to 'pick it up as they go'. They may well do this, but how many customers have you alienated in the process, and how many sales have you lost? This chapter looks at how you can motivate your staff to provide good customer service through training and coaching.

DEVELOPING YOUR STAFF

Training can cover a wide area and need not only be job or product specific but can also include training in interpersonal skills, core customer skills, team building, problem solving, developing creativity, leadership, management, or in something completely unrelated to the workplace. In order to be effective the training, whatever it might be, needs to help develop the individual to achieve his or her objectives and hence contribute towards achieving the organisation's objectives.

Training is a motivator.

DIFFERENT TYPES OF TRAINING

There are many different ways that training can be delivered and which method you use depends on the objectives for training, the employee, and the type and availability of training. There is:

- Classroom based training, either on site or off site
- Workshops
- Seminars
- Conferences
- Web based training
- On the job training
- Job shadowing
- Day release or night classes
- Coaching

Before deciding on which type or types of training to provide you need to weigh up the pros and cons for each type. Consider the cost, space, and time needed, as well as the return on investment, for each type of training.

PREPARING STAFF FOR TRAINING

Attitudes towards training vary. There are some people who see training as a punishment and indeed an insult. They believe they are attending a training course because the boss doesn't think they are capable of doing the job. There are others who are frightened of training, perhaps because it reminds them of school where they were unhappy, or where they struggled to learn. They are afraid that they will be made to look foolish. It is your task to understand how the individual feels about training and to fully discuss this with them.

Before undergoing any training the objectives for it need to be discussed, agreed and set. For example, why is this training being undertaken? What do the employee and the organisation hope to get out of it? How will what has been learnt be developed and put into practice in the workplace?

> You need to plan for good training, set and agree objectives and evaluate the training provided.

The employee must be fully involved in this process. Discuss with them what they believe their needs are; ask for ideas on how they can develop their skills, and suggest ways they could build on their skills and develop new ones. Link this with how it will not only benefit the employee as an individual but also the organisation. Ensure that progress is discussed and monitored on a regular basis.

IDENTIFYING TRAINING NEEDS

A **Training Needs Analysis** is an effective way to identify any gap between the skills your business needs and those your employees have. It involves gathering information to identify areas where your employees could improve their performance and then drawing up a personal development plan for each member of staff.

Some organisations feel that conducting a Training Needs Analysis is beyond their capabilities, or that they don't have the time or the objectivity to conduct one. In this case calling in an external consultant can help. There might also be government grants available in your region to help with this.

You can use employee surveys, management observations, customer comments, company meetings and inspections to collect information about training needs.

EXAMPLE

A new Managing Director was appointed to a company selling boats and marine equipment. He could see that productivity was not as high as it should be and that sales staff were underperforming. He conducted a staff survey, which showed that staff felt under-developed and neglected. Training had previously been available but it had been conducted on an ad-hoc basis with no proper evaluation of whether it supported the business goals. He set up a focus group made up of managers from each department and began with a review of current training, coupled with an analysis of what skills the company needed in the light of the corporate objectives. This allowed him to identify skill gaps and areas for improvement. At the same time the staff were interviewed to explore their personal goals and the types of training that would be appropriate for them, and the different parts of the business. Following this a personal development plan was drawn up and agreed with each member of staff with a timetable and budget and ongoing review and monitoring.

ACTION POINT

Look at your business goals – what skills will be required to meet these goals?

Evaluate who you want to train and what the best methods would be to train them, taking into consideration their preferences and circumstances, and the organisation's circumstances and budgets.

What can your organisation provide in the way of in-house training, funding and time?

Assess which consultants or training providers can fill in these gaps.

COACHING

Coaching is another form of ongoing staff development and training. Coaching is a way of instructing, directing, or assisting an employee to achieve a new goal. Coaching enables people to:

- Perform a new task
- Improve performance
- Develop a skill
- Solve a problem
- Build confidence

The skills you will need for good coaching are:

- Listening actively
- Asking questions
- Making suggestions
- Giving feedback

In order to conduct good coaching practices you need to create a partnership with the person you are coaching.

How to conduct a coaching session

The coaching session should be a completely separate meeting between the two people concerned and should be opened formally, for example: 'Jane, I'd like to begin our coaching session' or 'Is it all right if we begin our coaching session now?'

You need to agree the topic for coaching and ensure that longer term goals are achievable, timed and measurable. For each session you should also agree goals at the outset. For example: 'By the end of this session we will…'

Ensure that the seating arrangement is one of co-operation not hostility, ie you are not sitting on opposite sides of a desk or table, and ensure that your body language is open and your eye contact friendly. Take brief notes and listen actively. Share experiences where applicable. Ask open questions and give feedback. In addition, don't forget to set the date for the next session.

Things to avoid while coaching

- **Don't** become involved in the employee's personal situation and lose objectivity
- **Don't** follow your own agenda
- **Don't** try to solve employees problems
- **Don't** be judgmental
- **Don't** try to prove a point
- **Don't** hold a point of view that you want to impose

How to be a sucessful coach

- Agree the topic with the employee
- Make sure the coaching session takes place in a calm, undisturbed environment
- Set a specified amount of time for the session
- Give a clear, brief description of the issue to be addressed
- Identify and agree the goals for coaching

- Promote discovery – get the employee to consider options and how to evaluate these options
- Help the employee to discover and learn for himself, to trial new methods
- Set parameters of how far the employee is to go for himself before checking with the coach
- Ask open questions, ensure they are non judgmental in tone and content
- Give feedback
- Get the employee to re-cap and then summarise what the employee has said to ensure understanding
- Set a timetable for the next session
- Empower the employee – make sure they are able to carry out what has been agreed and that they are not blocked by others within the organisation when doing so
- Offer follow up support where appropriate
- Regularly review

QUICK RECAP

- *Provide ongoing training to ensure you have knowledgeable and confident staff.*
- *Training is both a motivator and a means of communication. It can be job or product specific, or include training in interpersonal skills, core customer skills, team building, problem solving, developing creativity, leadership, management, or in something completely unrelated to the workplace.*
- *Training must help develop the individual to achieve his or her objectives and hence contribute towards achieving the organisation's objectives.*
- *There are many different ways that training can be delivered and which method you use depends on the objectives for training, the employee, and the type and availability of training.*
- *Be aware of the different attitudes towards training. Whilst some may welcome it and see it as a reward others will see it as a form of punishment.*
- *You need to plan for training to be successful, set and agree objectives and evaluate the training provided.*
- *Coaching is another form of ongoing staff development and can be used alongside training or as an alternative to it.*
- *In order to conduct good coaching practices you need to create a partnership with the person you are coaching.*
- *The coaching session should be a completely separate meeting between the two people concerned.*
- *Agree the topic for coaching and ensure that longer term goals are achievable, timed and measurable. Also agree goals for each session at the outset.*

CHAPTER 8

Measure, monitor and reward

If you have set and communicated standards for your staff, and agreed performance objectives with them then it follows that you need to measure and monitor performance against those objectives and standards. You also need to recognise and reward achievements in order to continually motivate staff towards providing exceptional customer service. This chapter examines some ways you can address this.

MONITORING PERFORMANCE BY STAFF APPRAISALS

You can monitor staff performance by giving regular staff appraisals. The appraisal is intended to help staff achieve their full potential and build towards providing a quality service. Appraisals identify opportunities for development and training to benefit the individual in their career and achieve maximum contribution to the organisation. They can also help to improve communication. Shared ideas and views lead to a better service for customers and a more motivated workforce.

An appraisal is a review of the employee's skills and knowledge related to the job, all of which is vitally important in delivering exceptional customer service. If properly conducted, appraisals should result in staff who are better directed and motivated

What can go wrong?

However, if you have not had formal training in how to appraise, appraisals can sometimes end up being worse than if you didn't do them at all.

> A performance appraisal is a two-way process providing a structured examination of a person's behaviour at work.

It is advisable to ensure that staff are trained in how to give appraisals and it is also recommended that all employees undergo some training on how to be appraised. This way everyone will get the maximum benefit from appraisals.

There are many things that can go wrong with giving a staff appraisal. Here are some of the things you should avoid when appraising a member of staff's performance.

- Telling not listening
- Concentrating on negative points
- Being defensive about yourself and the organisation

- Talking about 'attitude' and other unmeasurables
- Giving opinions about a person's character
- Having an 'I am right' and 'you are wrong' attitude
- Seeing appraisals as a tedious waste of time
- Failing to face up to and talk about real issues
- Failing to carry out promises or implement plans

Getting it right

Appraisals should be given yearly. You should always give the staff member time to prepare for them and you should thoroughly prepare yourself. These are not 'fly by the seat of your pants' interviews. You can't go in thinking 'I'll play this by ear, and make it up as I go along.' It is your employee's job that is under discussion, their career, so treat it seriously and with respect.

Some employees will feel nervous and apprehensive so you need to set the tone and atmosphere and put them at ease. They could also feel vulnerable, defensive and aggressive and some may be inclined to sit there in silence and simply endure the whole thing, believing it is a complete waste of time.

Your job is to encourage open and honest discussion. Make sure you are not itching to get away. Seek first to understand then to be understood. If you do have to give criticism then check that it is specific and not a personal attack. Be prepared and have all the facts to hand.

If you are giving criticism then get a response to it by asking the staff member for suggestions on how they can bring about a desired change. Then summarise and agree the action to be taken. When giving the appraisal interview think about how you can improve things for the employee and how you can develop their talents to the benefit of the organisation. Also ask them how they feel they can improve their performance and what more they can contribute to the organisation. Remember that employees who feel valued will give better service.

TOP TIPS

How to make an appraisal successful

- Create a relaxed, informal atmosphere
- Explain the procedures involved
- Get the member of staff to assess his performance first
- Use 'open questions' to get the discussion going – these begin with 'who, what, where, when, how and why'
- Give praise for work well done
- Point out areas for improvement and the reasons why
- Demonstrate how you think these areas can be improved
- Encourage
- Summarise from time to time
- Discuss future training needs and development
- Finalise the discussion by a quick overall review of the interview
- State what will happen to any action plans
- End the interview on a positive note

REWARDING STAFF

Rewarding staff does not always mean giving a pay rise. In fact there are many other ways you can show your appreciation for your staff when they have performed well.

Give praise where due. Make each individual feel valued.

You can reward staff by involving them in decision making, by seeking their opinions and listening to them.

ACTION POINT

Try out some of the rewards listed below to boost staff morale and improve customer service.

Here are some other ways to reward staff:

- Say, 'Thank you'
- Say, 'Well done'
- Give them responsibility for tasks or projects
- Coach them in new skills
- Provide them with training to improve their skills and personal development
- Involve them in setting goals and targets
- Involve them in changes that affect them and their departments
- Take them down the pub and buy them a drink!
- Buy them cream cakes!

QUICK RECAP

- *You can monitor staff performance by giving regular staff appraisals.*
- *The appraisal is intended to help staff achieve their full potential and build towards providing a quality service.*
- *Shared ideas and views lead to better customer service and a more motivated workforce.*
- *A performance appraisal is a review of the employee's skills and knowledge related to the job.*
- *Appraisals should be given yearly. You should always give the staff member time to prepare for them and you should thoroughly prepare yourself.*
- *Employees who feel valued will give better service.*
- *You can reward staff by giving praise, by involving them in decision making, and by seeking their opinions and listening to them.*

CHAPTER 9

Customer surveys

Nothing stays the same, your customers' views will change and so too will their needs and wants. The market for your products and services will also change over time and this will affect how you deliver good customer service. This chapter examines how to use surveys to examine your customers' needs on an ongoing basis in order to make sure you're still delivering what they want, and to stay ahead of the competition.

KEEPING IN TOUCH WITH YOUR CUSTOMERS

In order to continue to provide good customer service, you need to be attuned to the changing needs of your customers and your market. This involves constantly adapting what you are offering, how you offer it and how you deliver your services to meet or indeed exceed your customer demands.

You can do this by:

- Talking to customers on a regular basis
- Sending out questionnaires
- Leaving questionnaires and feedback forms in visible spots or enclosing them with products when sold
- Conducting a telephone survey
- Carrying out an exit poll when a customer leaves the store/hotel/ business premises
- Conducting an online survey via your website or by sending an email
- Using a pop-up website evaluation survey

You can even use a combination of the above.

Deciding what type of survey to conduct and when depends on your type of business and what you hope to achieve. It also depends on your customer base. For example, you might need to conduct an online survey to those customers who have purchased from you online, and at the same time a telephone survey to customers who have bought over the telephone, and an exit poll to those customers who purchased over the counter.

Conducting surveys

Conducting a survey to gauge your customers' views of your organisation, its products or services and to ascertain satisfaction levels should be carried out on a regular basis – at the very least annually. It can be done by in-house staff although engaging an independent agency is more likely to give you honest feedback because your customers might not like to be as frank with you as they would with a stranger.

There are sample surveys online that can help you draw up a suitable questionnaire, or you can purchase software to help you do this. Alternatively, you might like to consider asking university staff to assist you as part of their degree course. I once did this for an accountancy client of mine with great success. Not only did the firm benefit but the students also gained valuable practical project experience.

TOP TIPS

In addition to regularly surveying your customer's views on your service you might also wish to canvass their opinion of how your staff performed immediately after the customer purchased the product when the experience is fresh in the customer's mind.

ACTION POINT

Thinking about your organisation write down the best method of surveying your customers, and state when you are going to do this.

DESIGNING A SURVEY

When wording a survey you need to ensure that you get unbiased answers. You can do this by asking 'open' questions ie those questions that provoke an 'open' response. Open questions begin with the words:

- How
- What
- When
- Why
- Who
- Where

TOP TIPS

It is better to ask '*How* satisfied are you with the purchase you made?' rather than '*Are* you satisfied with the purchase you made?'

Be clear from the outset what you wish to achieve from the customer satisfaction survey. You are ultimately trying to collect information about what to change within your organisation to make the customer's experience better, and what to carry on doing which the customer likes. So ask: what do you need to measure and what specifically do you want to find out?

EXAMPLE

A hotel needed to determine customer satisfaction levels and find areas where they could improve. They put a customer feedback form in each bedroom and offered an incentive for the customer to complete it. All completed surveys are entered into a draw at the end of each month and a winner is selected. The winner receives a money voucher for a department store and a discount off their next booking at the hotel. The hotel particularly wanted to measure:

- *Where its customers come from – ie the customer profile: their background, geographical area and ages*
- *How the customer heard of the hotel*
- *How the customer found the booking process*
- *How the telephone was answered*
- *How the customer was greeted on arrival*
- *The customer's view of the cleanliness of the hotel public areas and the bedrooms*
- *The facilities provided*
- *The standard and choice of food*
- *The standard of the staff*

ACTION POINT

Write down your objective for conducting a customer satisfaction survey.

Now write down the areas you wish to measure.

Areas your survey should cover

The areas you should cover include:

- Service promptness
- Courtesy of staff
- Responsiveness
- Understanding of the customer's problem

You might also wish to ask specific questions about the staff who interact with the customer directly, for example: the responsiveness of the reception staff, or the courtesy and promptness of telephone operators.

In addition, you may wish to gather demographic information about the customer. For example:

- Where do you live/your business address?
- What type of business are you in?
- What is your position?
- What is your function/role-responsibilities?
- What types of product(s) do you use?
- What types of service(s) do you use?
- What is the frequency of your product/service use?
- What is your spending range on products/services?
- Gender
- Age range
- Income range

TOP TIPS

It is usually a good idea to start with some basic questions first. The easiest questions to answer should be at the beginning of the survey. The more complex and those requiring a comment answer towards the end of the survey.

DIFFERENT TYPES OF QUESTIONS

Ranking Questions

Ranking questions are where the customer is asked to give a ranking against the services or products provided. We have already looked at some of these in earlier chapters where you asked were to **rank** your staff and your premises on scale of 0 to 5. In these types of questions you give the customer a range of options to choose from and to rank accordingly.

Typical ranking systems used for these questions can include the following examples:

Rate the following on a scale of 1 to 5 where 5 = Excellent, 4 = Good, 3 = Average, 2 = Fair, 1 = Poor

Or: 5 = Very satisfied, 4 = Satisfied, 3 = Neutral/Not sure, 2 = Dissatisfied, 1 = Very dissatisfied.

Tick box/ranking questions

Here you have provided a range of answers (rankings) but are asking the customer to simply tick the relevant box. For example:

Please rate the following:	Excellent	Good	Average	Fair	Poor
Our support staff's customer service					
The staff's product knowledge					

Please rate the following:	Very satisfied	Satisfied	Neutral/ don't know	Dissatisfied	Very dissatisfied
Overall, how satisfied are you with ABC's customer service?					
Overall, how satisfied are you with ABC's customer support?					

Here are a few more examples of tick box/ranking questions:

XYZ Limited provides good customer service

(Strongly agree, Agree, Neutral, Disagree, Strongly disagree)

How often does XYZ's customer service exceed expectations?

(Very frequently, Frequently, Not Sure, Infrequently, Very infrequently)

To what extent does XYZ's customer service exceed expectations?

(To very great extent, To a great extent, To some extent, To little extent, To very little extent)

Compared to one year ago, is ABC's customer service:
(Better, Worse, Same)

One additional area you might like to measure is helpfulness, for example:

How helpful were our counter staff?
Excellent Good Average Fair Poor

Other areas could include:

- Friendliness
- Being easy to deal with
- Phone calls being returned quickly
- Ensuring that people answering the phone are polite
- Ensuring that people answering the phone are cheerful
- Knowledgeable operators
- Listening to the customer
- Attentive to customer complaints
- Prompt in dealing with customer complaints
- Efficient
- Attention to detail
- Access to technical support

Further questions where ranking can be used include:

How likely would you be to recommend us to a friend or colleague?
Likely Unlikely Never

How likely would you be to buy or use our service again?
Likely Unlikely Never

However, if you get the answer 'unlikely' or 'never' then you need to find out what has gone so wrong that the customer is strongly opposed to using or buying your company's product or services again. And why he feels unable to recommend you to others.

If you can use this opportunity to get genuine feedback, and then act on it you might have a chance of not only winning that customer back, but getting him to tell others how efficient and understanding you were once you knew of the problem, and how you went out of your way to put things right. So the questions above need to be followed up with comment questions.

Comment questions

Comment questions allow the customer to explain his reason for giving the ranking he did, be it positive or negative. For example:

How likely would you be to buy or use our service again?

Likely Unlikely Never

If you have answered 'unlikely' or 'never' we'd very much like to know why. Please tell us (below) of your experience to allow us to make sure this doesn't happen again

Further comment question examples include:

What did you like best about our customer service?

What did you dislike most about our customer service?

If there was one thing we could do to improve our service what would it be?

How could we improve our service?

TOP TIPS

Although you can combine these different types of ranking and tick box questions it is usually best to stick to one or two question structures throughout your survey to avoid confusing the customer.

EXAMPLE

Hotel Questionnaire

We would very much like to hear your views on the Welcome Hotel and appreciate your time in completing our customer survey. Your survey can be completed anonymously. However, if you wish to provide your name and address your survey will be entered in a draw where you could have the chance of winning a £25 gift voucher.

How did you hear of us? *(You could provide a list of options here for the customer to tick)* Please tick as appropriate:

- ❑ Recommendation
- ❑ Advertisement
- ❑ Internet search
- ❑ Magazine article
- ❑ Other (Please state)................................

2. How did you make your reservation? (Please circle as applicable) (*Or you could use the same tick box formula as above)*

    By telephone   By letter   Online via our website
    By email   On the day

3. How satisfied are you with the way your booking was handled? (Please circle as applicable)

    Very satisfied   Satisfied   Neutral/don't know
    Dissatisfied   Very dissatisfied

4. How satisfied are you with the friendliness of our staff? (Please circle as applicable)

    Very satisfied   Satisfied   Neutral/don't know
    Dissatisfied   Very dissatisfied

5. How satisfied are you with the courteousness of our staff? (Please circle as applicable)

   Very Satisfied Satisfied Neutral/don't know
   Dissatisfied Very dissatisfied

6. How did you find the range of meals offered? (Please circle as applicable)

   Excellent Good Average Fair Poor

7. How satisfied are you with the cleanliness of your room? (Please circle as applicable)

   Very satisfied Satisfied Neutral/don't know
   Dissatisfied Very dissatisfied

8. How likely are you to return to our hotel? (Please circle as applicable)

   Likely Unlikely Never

If you have answered 'unlikely' or 'never' to any of these questions we'd very much like to know why. Please tell us (below) of your experience to allow us to make sure this doesn't happen again

....

....

9. How could we improve our service?

....

10. How likely would you be to recommend us to others? (Please circle as applicable)

    Likely Unlikely Never

Now for some brief questions about you.

Name:

Address: *(this can be optional – but you can politely say that if they don't provide an address then they won't have the opportunity of being entered for your free prize draw or money vouchers)*

Age range (please circle as applicable)

18-30	31-45	46-60
60-75	Over 75	

Marital status:

Number of children:

Thank you for completing this questionnaire. It will be entered into our monthly draw and if your name is selected you will receive a £25 gift voucher.

ACTION POINT

Now draft a customer survey for your organisation. Test it on a couple of 'tame' customers if necessary and get their feedback before rolling it out to your customer base.

ANALYSING RESULTS

I have worked with organisations that have commissioned very expensive customer satisfaction surveys and when they have received and analysed the results haven't liked them one little bit and therefore have ignored them. Incredible I know, but it happens. So, firstly the most important thing to do after you have the results of the survey is to take notice of them. Of course, if everything is positive, you can feel very satisfied and pat yourself on the back, but please don't ignore the negative comments, after all it is these you really want to know about in order to improve your customer delivery experience and therefore win more business.

If you have captured demographic information you will also be able to analyse your data by customer type or segment and then compare what different types of customers think about your organisation. This can provide information on trends and differences by region and/or product.

TOP TIPS

Examine those areas where customers have been critical, ask why it went wrong, why the service or product hasn't met the customer's required standards. Then look at how you can improve things.

Investigate suggestions; improve your product and services in those areas that mean the most to your customers. Don't change what they most like. Give them feedback, tell them that their answers were appreciated and are being acted upon. Feedback can be to individuals if appropriate, or it can be by fixing the things that they tell you need to be fixed and then issuing a newsletter, press statement or email bulletin to notify customers of the improvements you have made.

Alter the way you deliver a service if necessary and introduce new services or products that your customers are demanding.

Good customer service starts with good recruitment

Ensure that you recruit the right of people for the right job. When recruiting employees to provide customer service, look for those who not only have functional expertise but also good intepersonal skills and the right attitude: skills and functional expertise can be taught.

QUICK RECAP

- *Nothing stays the same – your customers' views will change and so too will their needs and wants.*
- *Keep in touch with your customers and their views by regularly surveying them.*
- *When wording a survey you need to ensure that you get unbiased answers – ask 'open' questions.*
- *Be clear from the outset what you wish to achieve from the customer satisfaction survey.*
- *The easy questions should be at the beginning of the survey. The more complex and those requiring a comment answer towards the end of the survey.*
- *Act on the survey results – examine those areas where customers have been critical, and look at how you can improve things.*
- *Providing excellent customer service starts with recruiting the right staff.*

PART 2

TECHNIQUES FOR SUCCESSFUL CUSTOMER SERVICE

CHAPTER 10

Voice and telephone handling techniques

Dealing with the public is not for everyone. It takes a certain type of individual to handle the different personalities, the problems and the challenges this brings. Some will find it rewarding and stimulating, others too demanding. The people who deliver exceptional customer service need to have excellent interpersonal skills. Good training and on-going staff development will help to provide your organisation with confident individuals. This chapter examines the basic qualities staff need for delivering good customer service, and how staff can make the right first impression through their voice. It also explores good telephone handling techniques.

QUALITIES OF GOOD CUSTOMER SERVICE STAFF

Staff who deal with customers need:

- Enthusiasm
- Positive body language and a presentable appearance
- Good listening skills and the ability to interpret needs accurately
- The ability to ask the right questions and control a conversation
- An assertive manner and a positive attitude
- A tactful and helpful attitude
- An open mind about people
- Good self-esteem
- To be quick thinking
- To be approachable and well mannered
- To have excellent communication skills
- To be a good team player

It's quite a list!

GIVING OUT THE RIGHT IMPRESSION

Staff who deal with customers, whether it be face-to-face or on the telephone, give out an impression of the organisation. This impression is based on the following:

55% of the impression we make on other people is determined by what they SEE. This includes our colouring, appearance, posture, body language, facial expression, eye contact and handshake.

38% of the impression we make on others is determined by what they HEAR. How our voice sounds. Is it empathetic? Is it clear and assertive? Can the customer understand what we are saying? Do we have an accent that they can understand?

Only 7% of the impression we make on others is determined by the WORDS they hear.

So how you look, react and sound is more important than the words you are using, certainly initially. Once the conversation develops this impression can, of course, change.

If the first and only impression you make is through the telephone then that whole area of what we see – 55% – moves into what we hear.

55% ~~**SEE**~~
↓
38% **HEAR**

So that **93%** of the impression you give out is based on your voice.

> People will base their judgments on what you say, or rather what they think you say and how you say it!

TOP TIPS

Record your voice in order to become aware of how much or how little energy you transmit to others.

YOUR VOICE

Your voice transmits energy and the subtleties of voice are far greater than we think. We can read an enormous amount into the vocal tone of people in the first few seconds. Whether this is on the telephone or dealing with customers face-to-face your voice has to convey a great deal. Depending on your line of business and the circumstances your voice might need to sound:

- Sympathetic
- Assertive
- Understanding
- Patient
- Kind
- Reassuring
- Enthusiastic

And of course confident!

It's not what you say it's the way that you say it!
Enthusiasm is infectious; inject it in your voice.

So, how do you sound, particularly on the telephone? What kind of impression are you giving out to the customer?

ACTION POINT

Record your voice when in a conversation with someone. This can be either on the telephone or face-to-face depending on which area of customer service you work in. You might like to do both. Now play it back and listen to how you sound. Measure it against this checklist below to see if and how you need to improve it.

To gain an understanding of the impression your voice is giving to your customer tick the areas which you feel apply to you:

- ☐ **You feel unnatural when speaking and hear a different voice, usually higher than your normal conversational tone.**
  If your voice sounds high it might not carry as much authority as it should. If so then to lower the pitch of your voice, slow down when you speak so that each word sounds clearer. Keeping your body language still will also inject more authority in your voice.

- **You're an adult but your voice sounds adolescent.**
  This can apply in particular to women who speak in a 'little girl', slightly squeaky voice. If this is you then it could affect your credibility when dealing with customers, particularly difficult ones. Again the same tip applies as in the previous answer. You need to slow down your speech and lower your voice. If you practise keeping your head perfectly still when you speak then you will find that more authority comes through in your voice. Women move their heads more than men when they talk. Coupled with the fact that women usually have a higher pitched voice it can make them sound very young.

- **You speak with a very low voice and generally at one level in a monotone.**
  Generally speaking it is men who suffer more from this than women. Here you need to lift your voice, to put more enthusiasm in it. One way of doing this is to practise reading aloud, and especially to young children. Those of you who are regular readers to children know that if you do not add the characters' voices into your stories they will tell you that you are not doing it 'properly!'

- **Your voice is too quiet and people ask you to speak up even when you're talking in only a small gathering.**
  If you talk too quietly then customers (particularly the demanding ones) will walk all over you. You need to practise projecting your voice. Talk to the far wall in your bedroom at home, or to the plants in the garden. Think of the sound coming from inside your chest not the back of your throat.

- ❑ **You use fillers like 'um', 'right', 'you know,' 'basically', 'do you know what I mean?'**

  We are all guilty of using fillers at some time but if you overuse them it becomes very irritating to the listener and it weakens the power of what you are saying. How many fillers did you use in an ordinary conversation? Count them on the recording. Be honest. Ask a colleague or friend to tell you when you are using them. Develop an ear for them yourself and reward yourself when you are improving.

- ❑ **You sound flat and dull when speaking on the telephone or through a microphone or on a tape.**

  Again practice reading aloud to children. Another good exercise is to recite poetry or to sing with your head hanging down between your knees. I know it sounds crazy but it's good fun and the sound that will come from you is amazing!

- ❑ **Your voice gets tired and your throat hurts after speaking for 15 to 20 minutes.**

  This is because you are putting a strain on your throat. The voice is coming from the back of your throat and not from your chest. You will also probably find that your shoulders are tense. Do some relaxation exercises, loosen the shoulders, unclench and let your body go limp.

- ❑ **You have a strong regional accent and people often ask you to repeat what you've said.**

  There is nothing wrong in having an accent, most of us have one, but it's no good if the customer can't understand what you are saying. The telephone can exaggerate accents making them even more difficult to understand. Again, listen to your recording, which words or rhythms of speech are difficult to hear? You may need the honest opinion of a colleague in order to find the areas that are difficult for others to understand.

- ❑ **You finish your sentences on a high as if you are asking a question when you are actually stating a fact.**
  This is very common in some regional accents and in many young people. Unfortunately if you do it too often it weakens the power of what you are saying. It sounds as if you are continually seeking someone's approval before proceeding with your speech. It can be as irritating as those fillers. Listen for it and try and correct it. Hearing it in others first may help you to hear it in your own patterns of speech.

- ❑ **You simply don't like the sound of your voice.**
  I've rarely met anyone who, when asked directly, say they like the way they sound. What is it you don't like? Are you being realistic? Ask a friend or colleague for their opinion on how you sound. Be open minded about it and don't be offended. Identify the areas you need to work on to project the image you want.

Your voice and the telephone

> If you work on the telephone, handling customer queries and complaints, then how you sound is vitally important.

Because the telephone is a non-visual tool (ie the customer can't see you and you can't see him) your voice has to convey a great deal. The customer is making an initial judgment about your organisation based on how you sound. In addition, you are making an initial judgment on the customer by how he sounds. Both these judgments could be wrong and could lead to misunderstandings.

For example if the customer is abrupt and has a forceful voice you might leap to the conclusion he is being rude or aggressive when really this is just his manner. If you don't keep an open mind and accept this then you could be in danger of reacting in either a submissive manner towards him or aggressively.

Here are a couple of exercises you can do to strengthen and improve your voice:

- Sing in the shower or in the car to learn how to project your voice and inject it with enthusiasm and meaning.
- Think about your breathing. Learn to hold your breath for longer than you usually do, then exhale slowly.

HANDLING CUSTOMERS ON THE TELEPHONE

In addition to the above there are other problems associated with using the telephone when dealing with customers and potential customers.

- It is more difficult to establish rapport on the telephone because the face-to-face visual element is missing.
- The telephone is intrusive – you could be calling someone at an inconvenient time.
- People are more likely to jump more readily to wrong conclusions. This is because people hear what they want to hear, or they could misinterpret your tone of voice.
- Callers and customers are tempted to do other things whilst talking on the telephone, which will break concentration. The customer might not be listening to you and you might not be giving the customer your full attention. Therefore vital information could be lost.
- It is more difficult to communicate accurate information – people remember more of what they see than hear.

- You can be cut off at any time. You may have a bad line, or you may have trouble understanding the customer's accent.

Adopting good telephone practice

Here are some guidelines on good telephone practice. This can be adapted depending on your organisation's culture.

- Answer the telephone promptly – within three to five rings. If it does have to ring longer make sure you apologise for keeping the caller waiting.
- Start each call by saying who you are, your name, position or department.
- Establish and use the other person's name early in the telephone conversation.
- Ask open questions to find out what the caller requires. Open questions begin with: who, what, where, how, when and why.
- If the call is an enquiry regarding your services, or a request for a brochure then don't forget to ask how the customer heard of your organisation. Take full details and read back the name and address. Ask the customer to spell his/her name.
- Listen. Resist the temptation to interrupt.
- When listening demonstrate you are listening by making listening noises such as 'yes', 'really', 'I see'.
- Concentrate. Don't be tempted to do two things at once. Give the telephone conversation your undivided attention.
- Make notes and read back key points so that the caller knows you are being attentive.
- Be lavish in explaining what you are doing, especially if it involves a silence while the caller 'hangs on'.
- Use assertive behaviour to control the call. Stay assertive even when you don't feel like it and especially when dealing with an aggressive or submissive person.
- Finish by recapping exactly what it is you are going to do as a result of the telephone conversation.

- Smile, even though you can't be seen by the other person, if you smile it helps your voice to sound more assertive and friendly.
- Record details of the call, make sure any action promised is carried out, and follow up if necessary.

How to establish and build rapport

It is important to build rapport with the caller/customer as quickly as possible. Here are some ways you can do this.

Don't shout and don't talk too quietly

If you shout down the line the customer will be put off by too loud a voice. Conversely if you are too quiet he will walk all over you. The voice must convey a great deal. The first few seconds are vital for the right impression: warm, friendly, alert and wanting to communicate effectively.

Match the speed of their voice

Mirror/pace your voice with the customer. For example, if the customer is slower speaking, then slow down. If you continue to talk at them like a babbling idiot, or fire questions at them, they will feel intimidated. Likewise, if you are dealing with a more direct individual, then be direct back (but not rude).

Vary your pitch

The telephone drains 30% of the energy level in your voice. Therefore you must make it sound more enthusiastic. Make a conscious effort to lift your voice. One of the ways of doing this it to 'smile' while you are speaking.

Avoid anger

We all collect anger. Get rid of it in your voice. If you are angry, or have just handled a difficult customer on the telephone, then take a bit of time to settle down before you pick up the telephone again because your emotions will come through. Likewise, if you are depressed then you will sound depressed and the customer will get a bad impression of your organisation.

Body posture

Look and be alert. If your body is slouched your voice will sound slouched and couldn't-care-less. Imagine the other person sitting in front of you. How would you look then? Alert and interested, I hope. Keep your head up. This puts less pressure on your vocal chords. This is why telephone headsets are so useful, because they eliminate the need for you to crook the phone under your chin while speaking (very bad for your neck muscles and back). And if you want to sound more serious then keep your head and body still when you talk, this helps to invest your voice with more authority.

Body language

Use the same body language on the telephone as you would normally face-to-face. This enables the enthusiasm to come through in your voice. Stand up to take difficult calls; it gives your voice more authority.

QUICK RECAP

- *93% of the impression you give out is based on your voice.*
- *If you work on the telephone, handling customer queries and complaints, then how you sound is vitally important.*
- *Subtleties of voice are far greater than we think. We can read an enormous amount into the vocal tone of people on the telephone in the first few seconds.*
- *It's not what you say it's the way that you say it! Enthusiasm is infectious; inject it in your voice.*
- *Lower the pitch of your voice and slow down when you speak to make each word sound clearer.*
- *Keeping your body language still will also inject more authority into your voice.*
- *Vary the pitch and pace of your voice to sound interesting and enthusiastic.*
- *Practise projecting your voice and avoid using fillers such as 'you know'.*
- *Try not to finish your sentences on a high as if you are asking a question when you are actually stating a fact as it will weaken what you are saying.*
- *Record your voice in order to become aware of how much or how little energy you transmit to others.*
- *Good telephone practice includes answering the telephone promptly, apologising for keeping the caller waiting, announcing who you are, and establishing and using the other person's name early in the telephone conversation.*
- *Smile – even though you can't be seen by the other person, if you smile it helps your voice to sound more assertive and friendly.*
- *Mirror/pace your voice with the customer. Vary your pitch and make sure you do not sound dull.*

CHAPTER 11

Appearance and body language

We've learnt that first impressions count, so having an acceptable appearance and giving out the correct body language signals to customers are vital. This chapter examines how to do this.

APPEARANCE

How you look, your clothes, personal grooming and hygiene all play a part in creating an impression not only of you, but also of your organisation. If you look dishevelled then people will think your organisation is shoddy. If you look sloppy then the impression of your organisation will be one of inefficiency.

There is a vast choice when it comes to deciding what to wear to work and unfortunately some people lack dress sense and can wear inappropriate clothing in the workplace without even realising it. This is why many customer facing staff have a uniform – it reduces the room for error, and it presents a corporate image, one that the organisation wishes to communicate to its customers.

Uniforms can also be worn for practical reasons – nurses wear a uniform not only so that the patients can easily identify them but also because it can often be a messy job, and it saves them getting their own clothes dirty. Uniforms can take the worry out of deciding what to wear to work. They can also save the wearer money.

Women can make more mistakes in their dress code than men.

When it comes to deciding what to wear to work, women tend to make more mistakes than men because they have more choice: trousers, jeans, shorts, skirts, dresses, jumpers, T-shirts, low cut tops, the list is endless, whereas men are more limited in their choice. That doesn't mean to say they don't make mistakes. We have all seen sloppily and inappropriately dressed men at work as well as women.

If a woman wears a tight fitting, very short skirt, and clinging top, or a dress with a low cut, what are the signals she is giving out to customers? Is this the message you want conveyed for your organisation? If a man or woman is wearing faded and patched jeans again think about the message this is conveying. In some industries this might not matter. Does it matter in yours?

> It is up to you and your organisation to decide what is an appropriate form of dress.

If a staff member has a problem with hygiene then this must be dealt with tactfully. However, rather than telling someone that their hair looks awful, and they should go home and wash it, perhaps on a day when they have washed it you could compliment them! People respond much better to praise than to criticism.

If you don't deal with a delicate situation, like a hygiene or dress problem, as soon as it arises, then it will only make you feel awkward and even resentful towards that staff member. This will show in your body language and behaviour, and in turn make that individual surly and resentful.

Body piercing and tattoos can be another thorny topic. If you have clearly stated your policy on a suitable dress and appearance code at an interview, and it is written in the staff handbook, which the staff member has seen, and he has received a proper induction, then there shouldn't be a problem with this.

BODY LANGUAGE

> How you project yourself through your body language is vitally important.

You may be speaking the right words, but if your body language is communicating a different message then it is that message that your customers will react to.

TOP TIPS

Non-verbal signals are at least four and a half times as effective as verbal signals and facial expressions are eight times as powerful as the words used.

We look at someone a third of the time we are talking to them and this look can convey anything from boredom and irritation to enthusiasm and liking. If you are in a situation where you are annoyed with (or don't like) the customer in front of you then your body language could betray your emotions. You might begin to fidget, look bored, avoid eye contact, or glance at your watch, all of which will only serve to make that customer even more awkward or angry. Front line staff need to know how to control their emotions and the advice in this book on a positive inner voice (p157) will help them to do so. You need to keep an open mind and open your mind about people.

You can also enhance the image you project, and your feelings of self-confidence, by deliberately using more positive body language. Positive body language will send positive messages to your brain, which in turn will send even more positive messages back to your body language.

People will pick up on this and will therefore act more positively towards you.

Positive body language

↓

Positive messages to the brain

↓

More positive body language

↓

Customer reacts to positive body language from the member of staff

Positive body language signals

Having a good posture will help. Good posture is about the natural alignment of the head and spine with the body. Posture is governed by habit and can be difficult to change. The chin thrust forward is fairly typical of an aggressive, go-ahead personality. Someone who is deaf in one ear will listen extra hard with the other ear and will tilt their head forward. A short podgy person who habitually slumps will draw attention to his/her size. Fashions can affect posture – for example high heels and tight skirts will throw the body forward and restrict movement. The body feels differently in different clothes and this will affect your posture. Try to keep your posture upright, your shoulders back and your chin up (but not too high).

> Having a good posture will help you feel more confident and self-assured and able to deal with your customers in an assertive manner.

Positive body language

- Keep your head up and your shoulders back and relaxed. Stand up straight not hunched over. Think of a piece of string pulling you up from the top of your head.
- When sitting in front of the customer try linking your hands together in front of you on the desk, as though to form a steeple, this can prevent you making nervous mannerisms. It also suggests confidence and self-possession.
- Stillness suggests ease and comfort in a situation, especially the ability to keep hands and feet still and relaxed. Don't fidget.
- Sit upright and alert.
- Give your customer good eye contact.
- Gestures showing open palms of hands demonstrate openness and confidence.

- Sitting asymmetrically demonstrates confidence and is less threatening to the other person than sitting face on, especially if it is across a table or desk.
- Leaning forward indicates interest, but don't move too close or you could be intimidating your customer by invading their personal space.
- When standing, keep your hands and arms relaxed at your side. Don't fold your arms, it is a closed gesture and can look threatening and defensive.
- If you need to take notes try not to do so constantly. Jot down key points and then give your customer regular eye contact.
- Turn your body to the speaker/customer and look interested in what they are saying. Tell yourself that you *are* interested, as it will show on your expression. If you are thinking 'this person is boring the pants off me', then your expression will reflect this.
- When listening, keep your body open, arms leaning forward on the table, hands gently folded.

Negative body language signals

Nervous mannerisms including nail biting, finger and foot tapping, playing with hair, or adjusting clothing, smoothing eyebrows could all be construed as negative body language signals and should therefore be avoided. In addition, playing with objects and personal effects (wedding rings, pencils etc). often indicates tension.

Pointing at people, waving your fist, thumping the table, all show aggression and tension. Hopefully you won't be doing any of this, although your customer might be!

Touching the face is associated with negative emotions – guilt, self-doubt, and irritation. Likewise touching the chin and mouth shows doubt, a reluctance to speak or accept what is being said. It can also portray lying. Touching the nose is also said to be an indication of lying; touching the eye not liking what you are seeing or not wanting to see any further, and touching the ears: not liking what you are hearing.

EXAMPLE

It is very easy to adopt negative body language signals through force of habit and not be aware of the signals you are giving out. I once worked with a woman who, when she spoke, always covered her mouth with her hand. This was weakening the power of what she was saying, and often giving the impression that she was lying. When I asked her about this she confessed that it was a habit she'd adopted when younger because she was very self-conscious that her skin was bad and she used her hands to cover up her acne.

ACTION POINT

Try video role plays with your staff putting them in various situations with customers and then replay it to see what body language signals they are giving out. Get the staff member to identify what he or she thinks is weak body language, (communicating a negative message) and say how they feel they can improve this.

BODY LANGUAGE AND CUSTOMER SERVICE

Greeting the customer

When greeting the customer the first impression is vitally important. The body language signals are:

- The handshake
- Eye contact
- The smile

Your handshake

Whether or not you shake hands with customers is dependent on your type of organisation, the situation you are in and the sector in which you operate. If you or your staff shake hands with customers then make sure your handshake is giving the correct impression. The handshake also creates a good opportunity to establish a rapport.

Your handshake can say a great deal about you. A firm dry handshake reveals confidence, professionalism and status. If you have a weak handshake it will convey the impression of a weak person, even if you aren't.

What is your handshake like? Try shaking hands with someone you know and ask them for their honest opinion. If you need to firm it up then practise it.

> **TOP TIPS**
>
> When you shake hands take the whole hand in a firm gip, not just the fingers. Be aware of the other person's handshake and if it is not as strong as yours then weaken yours a little to help build rapport. If it is stronger than yours, try not to wince. Just return the pressure slightly.

Always offer your hand first and invariably the other person will take it. Your elbow should be tucked into your waist when you shake hands and not outstretched.

The handshake is a fairly universal greeting but if you are working with customers from different cultures please be aware that this might not be their normal form of greeting. A nod and smile should suffice.

Good eye contact

There are cultural differences in how much eye contact to give the other person when meeting them and listening to them. In Britain, America, Australia and Canada quite a lot of eye contact is given between individuals. In Europe less so, although research has shown the Greeks prefer a considerable amount of eye contact, the Swedes less so. Arabs are fairly dependent on maintaining eye contact whilst the Japanese tend to look downward aiming at a person's neck rather than directly into their eyes.

When you meet someone you should aim to hold the eye contact whilst smiling and shaking hands with them and then break eye contact when the other person looks away, or when you finish shaking hands and change your body posture.

Too much eye contact can make the other person feel uncomfortable. It can be used as a dominant gesture and is an invasion of privacy. If you give too little eye contact it can suggest boredom, lack of interest or maybe shyness. Closing the eyes completely when making conversation is a negative signal and should be avoided.

If the person refuses to give you eye contact then try asking a direct question. Once you get eye contact no matter how fleeting, connect with it and smile to show encouragement and to build rapport.

The smile

Your smile should be warm and welcoming. Obviously the better you know and like someone the warmer your smile. We all know, or have met people though, who are smiling but their eyes show no warmth or welcome and the gesture is an empty one. False smiles are held in place, the lips stiff and stretched and the eyes stay unsmiling. This is also often an aggressive and sometimes dominant stance and can be used as a gesture to keep people at their distance.

Personal Space

Personal space is the space around us that we feel comfortable with. We only allow those close to us to invade that space. If others do invade, uninvited, then we feel threatened by it and wish to step back. Make sure you are not invading your customers' personal space. Different cultures have different distances so be aware of this. British people are usually comfortable at a distance of about three feet.

QUICK RECAP

- *Staff who deal with customers give out an impression of your organisation.*
- *How you look plays an important part in creating an impression.*
- *How you project yourself through your body language is vitally important.*
- *Non-verbal signals are said to be at least four and a half times as effective as verbal signals, and facial expressions eight times as powerful as the words used.*
- *We look at someone a third of the time we are talking to them and this look can convey anything from boredom and irritation to enthusiasm and liking.*
- *You can enhance the image you project and your feelings of self-confidence by deliberately using more positive body language.*
- *Your handshake can say a great deal about you. A firm, dry handshake reveals confidence, professionalism and status.*
- *Personal space is the space around us that we feel comfortable with; don't threaten others by invading their personal space.*
- *Try to keep your posture upright, your shoulders back and your chin up.*
- *Eye contact and a smile are important parts of welcoming customers and showing you are interested.*

CHAPTER 12

Listening

One of the key skills required by staff who deal with customers is that of listening. We all think we listen well, but many of us don't. This chapter examines the different types of listening and how you can improve your listening skills.

WHAT DO YOU KNOW ABOUT LISTENING?

Try this quick questionnaire to find out how much you know about listening. Answer either true or false to the following questions:

1. Most people listen more than they speak
2. Good listeners don't say anything while they listen
3. Good listeners look at the speaker
4. People listen well when they feel strongly about the topic
5. Listeners are more influenced by how something is said than by what is actually said
6. People listen to criticism

Now examine the answers to see how many you got right.

Answers:

1. *Most people listen more than they speak*: **True**

   Yes, there are more people who listen more than they speak, yet we all know those individuals who like the sound of their own voice and who never give anyone a chance of having their say. And, although we might listen, how much of that is quality listening, or how much simply drifts in one ear and out of the other? When dealing with customers you need to be fully attuned to what they are saying, not only listening to the words they are speaking but also to the underlying meaning behind the words. You can do this by observing their body language while they are speaking, and listening to the actual words (vocabulary) they are using.

2. *Good listeners don't say anything while they listen:* **False**

   Good listeners, while not actually speaking will make the 'listening noises' when they listen, eg 'uh huh', 'I see', 'really'. This helps to confirm to the speaker that they are genuinely listening. This is particularly important when dealing with customers on the telephone otherwise the customer will hear a long silence and will then be forced to ask 'Are you still there?' or will say, 'Have you been listening?'

3. *Good listeners look at the speaker:* **True**
   Good listeners *always* look at the speaker; it is the simplest way to show that you are truly listening. Have you ever been on the end of a conversation where the person listening looks away, or beyond you? Or with someone who asks you a question and then looks away just as you answer it? How did you feel? Pretty cross and upset. When looking at the speaker keep your expression open, interested and concerned, this way you are signalling to them that they have your full attention.

4. *People listen well when they feel strongly about the topic:* **False**
   People do not listen well when they feel strongly about a topic because their own feelings get in the way. They are just waiting for the speaker to finish so they can jump in and give their views.

EXAMPLE

Think about a conversation you've had in the past, with a friend or colleague when discussing something that you have strong views about – how quickly did you jump in with your opinion? Was it before they even finished speaking? When the other person was speaking were you really listening or was your mind racing to put forward your experience or views?

5. *Listeners are more influenced by how something is said rather than by what is actually said:* **True**
   Think about the great speakers or those personalities on television who you find persuasive. It is not so much the actual words they are speaking but the way they say them that influences you. If they used the same words but put no meaning,

passion or enthusiasm into them then you would soon become bored and stop listening. Do you remember what we covered in the previous chapter? 38% of the way we communicate is through our voice, how it sounds is often more important than what is being said.

6. *People listen to criticism:* **False**

   We do not listen well to criticism because our personal feelings get in the way. While we are being criticised or blamed we are often thinking, 'how dare they?' We become upset and indignant. We all think our own view is the real one. It is not. Keeping an open mind and focusing on the specific criticism and telling ourselves that it is not directed at us personally but at the problem can help. This will be covered more fully in chapter 14 (p.147).

TOP TIPS

When you are having a conversation with another person, receive what he or she has said before rushing in to make your contribution. If you feel you want to interrupt, think about pausing and breathing before you start to talk. A pause before you speak can also add significance.

TWO TYPES OF LISTENING

Listening is an essential part of being a good communicator and being good at delivering customer service. As more and more of our communication becomes visually (ie the internet) and text based we are forgetting how to listen.

Listening involves both the ability to understand what is being said, and the ability to organise and analyse the messages in order to retain them for subsequent use.

There are two types of listening:

1. Casual listening
2. Critical listening

Casual listening

Casual listening is what we tend to do most of the time. We are only half listening, we retain bits of the conversation and we discard other parts of it. As a result you often get the following scenario between two people:

'Don't forget that order is due in today.'

'Is it? You didn't tell me.'

'Yes, I did, two days ago. You weren't listening.'

Critical listening

Critical listening requires concentration and stamina. Here you are making a real effort to understand the other person's point of view. You are listening to them, retaining what they say, storing it away and then retrieving some of it later when you need it. These skills are essential in a customer service situation.

So what stops us listening?

There are many things that prevent us from listening not least of which is laziness. We simply can't be bothered. Or maybe we've never been trained to listen. Perhaps our upbringing is such that no one has listened to us so why should we listen to them?

Here are some of the things that prevent us from listening:

Physical tiredness or discomfort

We may be tired or hungry. We may be hot or cold. We may be under stress and feel anxious or unwell.

Distractions and mind wandering

We may be distracted because of a noise. Or we may be thinking ahead of all the things that need to be done. We may be worried about someone or something.

Reactions to the speaker

We may dislike the person who is talking to us. We may find them boring or opinionated.

Preconceived ideas

We may have preconceived ideas about the person we are communicating with. Perhaps we have been told that this particular customer or group of customers are awkward and difficult. This will influence how we then handle them.

EXAMPLE

This has happened to me many times in the course of my career when running a training course, giving a seminar, or going to a meeting. I've been pre-warned that a certain person is really difficult to deal with. If I allow this to colour my view of that person then I could go into the meeting really worried about dealing with them. I might react aggressively by thinking, 'They won't get the better of me,' and jump in with my view before they have even had the chance to speak! Or I might be thinking, 'What if I can't handle them?' and therefore I might behave submissively giving out a poor impression and allowing myself to be walked all over.

What usually happens is the 'difficult person' is no trouble at all. They are not difficult with me, not because they've suddenly changed overnight but because I have not allowed any preconceived ideas to interfere with the way I have communicated with them. I have kept an open mind and tried to listen to them and understand where they are coming from.

Strong emotions and prejudices

We inherit prejudices and beliefs from our parents, guardians, teachers, religious leaders, friends and many others. Perhaps we have been 'conditioned' not to like or understand people who are from a different culture. Perhaps we have been 'conditioned' to believe we are superior to others because of our education or social standing. Or we may be prejudiced towards someone because of his or her gender or his or her size. If this is the case then we take those prejudices with us when we meet someone face-to-face and these prejudices can influence the whole exchange between you and that person, and, as a result, you may be patronising or hostile towards them.

It is hard to clear your mind of prejudices before meeting someone because instinctively we try and 'place' people in order to give us a framework for reacting with them, but that framework can be very wonky to begin with.

Different perspectives

We see things differently to the person talking and we disagree with them. This will influence the whole way we react with them.

Desire to talk

Many of us love to talk most of the time, to be the centre of attention; we love the sound of our own voice and think that only our opinions really count. This prevents us from listening. To be a good listener we must cease to be self-absorbed and become genuinely interested in the other person.

ACTION POINT

Exercises for improving listening skills

1. Take five minutes a day to sit quietly somewhere, close your eyes and listen to all the sounds around you. Become conscious of them. How many different sounds can you hear? In addition to improving your listening skills this can also be relaxing.
2. Listen to the radio as much as possible, talk programmes, not music. What information did you receive? Can you summarise it?

TOP TIPS

For successful listening skills

Start listening with the first word and then listen intently

Stop what you are doing and listen – don't be tempted to do two things at once

Turn off all negative thoughts you have about the person speaking

Think at the speed they're talking, don't jump ahead

Do not interrupt

Judge the content and not the delivery

Suspend your judgment and keep an open mind

Resist distractions if you possibly can

QUICK RECAP

- *Listening is an essential part of being a good communicator and therefore essential to customer service.*
- *Listening involves:*
  - *the ability to understand what is being said*
  - *the ability to organise and analyse the messages in order to retain them for subsequent use.*
- *There are two types of listening: casual listening and critical listening.*
- *There are many reasons why we don't listen properly: physical tiredness or discomfort, desire to talk, different perspectives, strong emotions and prejudices, preconceived ideas, reactions to the speaker, and simple distractions and our mind wandering.*
- *It takes practice and concentration to listen properly.*

CHAPTER 13

Questioning and interpreting needs

In addition to listening to the customer you also need to be able to interpret their needs accurately. In order to do this you will need to ask the correct questions, control and direct the conversation. This chapter shows how you can do this.

UNDERSTANDING A CUSTOMER'S NEEDS

Not everyone is good at expressing themselves, in fact many people aren't. The customer may believe he has told you exactly what he is looking for or what the problem is but you simply didn't understand him. This could be because he hasn't explained it clearly. Alternatively, the customer might be requiring something that needs your expert advice and in order to give this you need to direct the conversation and probe for more information to help you provide that advice.

TOP TIPS

In order to deliver exceptional customer service, whether it is on the telephone or face-to-face, there are two things you need to remember from the customer's perspective: 'I am important' and 'Consider my needs'.

Making the customer feel valued and important is a critical step in providing exceptional customer service. So how do you do this?

In order to make people feel important you need to get them to talk, to open up, and in order to consider their needs you need to ask the correct questions, listen and interpret what they are saying. Only by doing this will you be able to identify their needs and deliver the correct service or product to fulfil that need.

EXAMPLE

The customer wishes to purchase a computer but isn't sure which one to buy. He comes to you, the sales assistant, for help. In order to satisfy his needs and find the correct computer for him you need to ask him some questions; only then can you show him the range of computers on sale that might suit his requirements. In order to probe those needs you need to ask 'open' questions.

QUESTIONING TECHNIQUES

Open questions are those that require an answer other than simply a 'yes' or 'no'.

Open questions

Open questions begin with the following words:

- What
- Where
- When
- How
- Why
- Who

By beginning your conversations with these words you will get even the most reluctant of people to open up.

Open questions will help you to:

- Properly understand what the customer wants
- Make the customer feel important
- Control the conversation
- Understand the customer's needs

You may think that you already use open questions but many people don't and instead they resort to asking **closed questions**, which, of course, are designed to close the conversation or to narrow it to a certain field, or confirm a diagnosis of the need.

Closed questions usually elicit a single word response, 'yes' or 'no'.

Closed questions

These types of questions begin with:

- Is/Are
- Should/Shall
- Could/Can
- Will/Would
- Do/Did

EXAMPLE

So taking our above example the sales assistant can ask 'open' questions to find out exactly what the customer is looking for and 'closed' questions to narrow the conversation and confirm he is interpreting the need correctly. He could therefore conduct the conversation as follows:

Sales Assistant: *'**What** are you intending to use the computer for, sir?' **(open question)***
Customer: *'I run a small voluntary organisation and I want something to help me with my correspondence and to do my budgets.'*

The sales assistant can probably judge from this that the customer doesn't want a gaming computer but something that can be used for small business/home use.

Sales Assistant: *'Do you need to take the computer away from home, perhaps on business or on holiday?' **(closed question)***
Customer: *'No. I only want to use it in my small study.'*

The sales assistant could therefore judge that the customer would prefer a desktop computer rather than a laptop computer. But rather than assuming this the good sales assistant would explain the options without confusing the customer and without using jargon which would belittle him.

Sales Assistant: *'In that case, sir, you might be better off with a desktop computer rather than a laptop. The laptop computer you can use anywhere, for example in another room in your house, and you can take it with you outside the house, whereas the desktop one will be stationary and located in your study. How does that sound to you?'*

Here the sales assistant has also summarised the customer's needs as he sees it and has then asked an open question to check that he has understood the customer's needs.

If the customer is happy with this, the sales assistant can then say, 'I'll show you what we have in the desk top computer range and see if we can find something that fits your needs.'

Of course I have simplified the situation here to demonstrate the point. Once the sales assistant has the basic information he can then begin to ask more open questions to **probe** the customer's needs, for example:

Probing questions

Examples of probing questions could include:

- 'How often would you need to use your computer?'
- 'How frequently will you use the internet?'
- 'What sort of budget are you looking to spend?'
- 'How important is it for you to use graphics to display your budgets to others?'

By probing, the sales assistant can find the right solution for that customer and therefore make him a satisfied customer.

I will return to this and examine other types of questions in chapter 16 when I look at handling the difficult or complaining customer.

ACTION POINT

Next time you are at a party or at a business function, find someone new to talk to, ie someone you have not previously met. Set yourself a goal of finding out as much as you can about them. Resist the temptation to talk about yourself and ask them 'open' questions. This is an excellent way of practising your 'open' questioning technique.

TOP TIPS

Speaking to improve communication

Tailor what you say to the understanding of the receiver and the level of knowledge he or she already has.

Explain jargon.

Be logical in the presentation of what you say – as would appear logical to the receiver.

Speak in manageable chunks. No one should be expected to listen attentively non-stop for more than about five minutes.

Invite comment and feedback, if not offered spontaneously.

QUICK RECAP

- *In addition to listening to the customer you also need to be able to interpret their needs accurately.*
- *In order to do this you need to ask the correct questions.*
- *Open questions are those that require an answer other than simply a 'yes' or 'no'. They begin with 'What', 'Where', 'When', 'How', 'Why', 'Who'.*
- *Closed questions usually elicit a single word response, 'yes' or 'no'. They begin with 'Is/Are', 'Should/Shall', 'Can/Could', 'Will/Would', 'Do/Did'.*
- *Both sorts of questions are needed to elicit different types of information, enabling you to deliver service that meets your customer's needs.*

CHAPTER 14

Assertiveness

In order to provide successful customer service you and your staff need to behave assertively. This is sometimes easier said than done, particularly under difficult circumstances. Why? Because we are not born assertive: it is something that we need to learn. This chapter defines assertiveness and shows how you can deal with customers in a more assertive manner.

UNDERSTANDING BEHAVIOUR

Human beings are primed to behave in a certain way when faced with danger, or when threatened. Our natural reflexes mean that we will either want to run away from danger, or attack whoever is causing it before it gets us. This is known as the **flight or fight response** and can be translated into us either behaving submissively (flight) or behaving aggressively (fight).

In today's society, however, it is not acceptable that we behave in this manner. If we do then we could end up in trouble with the law. It certainly isn't acceptable behaviour when dealing with customers. Furthermore, behaving aggressively is bad for your health resulting in an increased heart rate, which can lead to high blood pressure, and therefore the possibility of heart attack and strokes. And behaving submissively leads to low self-worth and a lack of confidence, which in turn can result in greater exposure to viruses, infections and depression. I examine later in this chapter what is meant by aggressive, submissive and assertive behaviour.

> Behaving assertively therefore benefits us as individuals and also benefits our customers.

WHAT DOES ASSERTIVENESS MEAN?

An assertive person has the confidence to express opinions whilst respecting the rights of others. It is someone who is keen to reach solutions to conflicts that give satisfaction to both sides. An assertive person will listen to the customer and will not impose his views. They will, however, stand their ground if they need to in a non-threatening manner. Their body language is confident and open, and their eye contact good.

An assertive person has:

- A positive attitude
- An open mind about people
- Good self-esteem and confidence
- An approachable manner

Assertive behaviour enables us to deal with difficult people and situations more confidently.

Before we examine how to behave assertively towards customers let's just take a closer look at submissive and aggressive behaviour.

WHAT DOES SUBMISSIVE BEHAVIOUR MEAN?

Submissive behaviour means neglecting to defend your personal rights and beliefs.

If you act submissively you put the rights of others before your own rights. You constantly give in to demands and requests when you shouldn't and then you feel very upset about it. You find it difficult to communicate with awkward and demanding customers. You back down in situations where you should have stood your ground. You may also find yourself blaming others for mistakes that you have made, or blaming the company policy. You refuse to take calls in case they might be from demanding customers and you make promises that you can't keep just to get the customer off your back and then leave your colleagues to clear up the mess!

What makes us become submissive?

We can become submissive when we are under attack (the flight syndrome) or even when we think we are going to be attacked.

This doesn't necessarily require a physical assault, a verbal one can also prompt the fight or flight syndrome. We can become submissive when faced with a bullying boss, partner, parent, customer or someone else in an authoritative position.

Submissive individuals usually have low self-esteem, which can sometimes, but not always, be formed as a child. If you are told that you are useless, too fat, too tall, too thin, too clumsy this is how you will end up seeing yourself and your self-worth will be dented.

If confronted by an angry, over-confident or demanding customer we cannot afford to run away, or simply capitulate. We need to handle them in an assertive, confident manner. This is not always easy. I look at how to do this in chapter 16.

First though examine your own behaviour – are you behaving submissively? Take a look at the list of questions on p.151 and answer either yes or no to each one to see if you are behaving submissively.

CHANGING YOUR BEHAVIOUR

How can you change submissive behaviour into assertive behaviour?

TOP TIPS

Given that submissiveness can be caused by a lack of self-esteem telling yourself what you are good at and focusing on your positive traits rather than any negative ones will help you become more assertive.

Good training will also give you confidence. This should include product training and training in techniques to deal with different types of customers.

I am always apologising when I don't need to be Yes/No

I have difficulty in making requests and go about it in a roundabout way Yes/No

I am quietly spoken Yes/No

I find it difficult holding eye contact with another person Yes/No

I try not to be noticed in meetings or gatherings Yes/No

I fidget unnecessarily Yes/No

I have difficulty in speaking my mind Yes/No

I don't like rocking the boat but prefer to keep things as they are, even if I don't like them Yes/No

I have difficulty in expressing my feelings Yes/No

When I do say 'no' I feel guilty Yes/No

How honest have you been with your answers? If you have answered 'yes' to all or most of the questions then your behaviour is submissive. Perhaps you could ask a friend or colleague, someone whose opinion you respect and trust, to answer these questions about you and then compare and discuss your answers.

ACTION POINT

1. List your strengths/positive assets/what you like about yourself. If you have difficulty doing this then ask a trusted friend or colleague to write down what they like about you.
2. Put your list on a board near your desk or in your locker. In fact anywhere you can see it or quickly check it when feeling low, or after handling a particularly difficult or upsetting event.
3. Look at it every morning to help you focus on the positive things about you rather than the negative.
4. Say your positive traits out loud to yourself. Your brain will then send positive signals to your body language which will become more open and assertive. Others will then react to this in a more assertive manner when communicating with you.
5. When you are feeling negative, or someone has said something negative to you, or you've had a difficult experience, revisit this list and remind yourself of your good points.

TOP TIPS

If you deal with a particularly difficult customer or a query that you didn't resolve to your satisfaction then discussing it with a supervisor, manager or mentor can help. Ask how you could have dealt with it in a more assertive manner and learn from your mistakes.

WHAT DOES AGGRESSIVE BEHAVIOUR MEAN?

Aggressive behaviour means that you consider your rights and beliefs are more important than the other person and you say so.

Aggressive people can also behave in an underhand and manipulative manner to get their own way. If you act aggressively then you refuse to let the customer finish explaining what it is he wants, or what the problem is. You interrupt him and look exasperated, or hostile. Your body language is closed. Your voice is terse and abrupt. You might resort to using put downs, for example, 'Well what did you expect for the money!'

What makes us become aggressive?

Apart from being threatened or in danger of attack and adopting the fight response people often become aggressive, or use aggression, because it gets them results. Sometimes it can be a form of behaviour that has been learnt from childhood. For example if the child screaming its head off in the supermarket is rewarded with a bag of sweets to keep it quiet then the message that is being sent to that child is one of behave badly and you will be rewarded! The child will carry on behaving badly because it has seen that this type of behaviour gets it what it wants.

Some people also behave aggressively because it gives them a sense of power and sometimes it covers up for their own insecurity. Then there are others who come across as being aggressive because they are trying too hard to assert themselves. Some people end up acting aggressively because they do not have the education or the vocabulary to adequately express how they feel. And some people think that behaving aggressively *is* a form of behaving assertively.

So examine your own behaviour – are you behaving aggressively? Take a look at the list of questions on p.154 and answer either yes or no to each one to see if you are behaving aggressively.

I believe in delivering instructions and commands and see no need to consult others	Yes/No
Being in control is very important to me	Yes/No
I tend to use sarcasm sometimes as humour and sometimes to make a point	Yes/No

When I am upset I can hold a grudge for a long time afterwards Yes/No

When I am upset I fly off the handle too quickly Yes/No

I get very impatient with people who can't make up their minds Yes/No

People who are too slow irritate me Yes/No

How honest have you been with yourself? Do you need to get someone else to answer these questions as they see you? If so what results did they come up with? If you have answered mainly yes, then beware you are behaving aggressively.

Changing your aggressive behaviour

To change your behaviour from being aggressive to being assertive, firstly you will need to recognise and accept that your behaviour is aggressive. This can sometimes be the biggest barrier to overcoming predominantly aggressive behaviour. You might not realise that this is how you are behaving; you might be confusing your aggressive behaviour with being assertive. Or you might wish to continue to use aggressive behaviour and simply not care about the impact it has on others. If so then working with customers is not for you.

Sadly, I have come across many people while training in customer service roles who see the customer as a nuisance, an inconvenience, stupid and irritating. To these people, and their bosses, I have suggested they get another job and get as far away from the customer as possible.

While aggressive people always think that only their rights, views and opinions matter and that everyone else is in the wrong, assertive people will accept that others have rights, views and opinions which, although they differ from their own, are just as valid.

ASSERTIVE BEHAVIOUR

To recap, an assertive person is someone who has the confidence to express their opinions whilst respecting the rights and opinions of others. It is someone who is keen to reach solutions to conflicts that give satisfaction to both sides.

So examine your own behaviour – are you behaving assertively? Take a look at the list of questions below and answer either yes or no to each one to see if you are behaving assertively.

What happens in my life depends on my own actions Yes/No

I don't bear a grudge, when something is over it's over and I don't think about it again Yes/No

I think getting ahead doesn't mean someone else has to lose out Yes/No

When something upsets me I prefer to talk about it and deal with it than bottle it up Yes/No

I don't feel embarrassed or anxious about expressing my feelings Yes/No

I think everyone is entitled to their own views, which might not be mine Yes/No

> Assertiveness is standing up for your own rights without violating the rights of others.

Having an open mind

This involves developing a positive inner voice. You may find yourself experiencing the following reactions when dealing with customers, we'll go through how to work on your inner voice and making sure that it is positive.

Aggressive inner voice

A customer who is continually complaining about your organisation's services is coming towards you. He is very difficult and demanding and you find dealing with him tough. This might be the dialogue that is going through your head:

'Oh, no, not him again! Why do I always get to deal with him? He's a real nuisance, a nightmare. He's always complaining. He's no right to behave like this to me. Who does he think he is?'

Your feelings are of frustration, anger, and impatience. If you don't correct this negative inner voice your behaviour will reflect those feelings and you will behave aggressively towards this customer. This will show in your body language and expression, and in your choice of words and your tone of voice. The customer will pick up on this behaviour and react in an even more aggressive manner; you clash and have a no win situation.

Submissive inner voice

Alternatively your inner voice might be saying something like this:

'Oh, no, not him again! Why does he always pick on me? Nothing I do is ever right. I find him so difficult to deal with. I know he'll shout and bawl at me and walk all over me. Help!'

Here you are going to end up being submissive, giving in to this man's every whim, letting him walk all over you – not very good for either you or the organisation.

So how should you change this to a more assertive response?

Getting an assertive and positive inner voice

First, recognise that your inner voice is wrong. It is negative in both the above scenarios. It is aggressive and defensive. Once you do this you then have the opportunity to change it to a more positive inner voice – something along the lines of:

'It's Mr Brown again. I know he is a difficult person to deal with, but I can handle him. I can keep calm, listen to what he has to say, and

deal with his queries and demands in a competent and professional manner. I am in control of the situation and myself.'

TOP TIPS

Getting a positive inner voice can help you to become more assertive and therefore handle those difficult situations and people more confidently.

I don't promise it will be easy at first, it takes a bit of practice, but with this kind of dialogue going through your head, your body language and posture will be more positive and you will project a more confident image, which in turn will communicate itself to the customer. In addition, keep your body posture upright and hold eye contact without glaring at the customer. If you drop your eye contact you automatically go into submissive mode. Try to use the customer's name, it helps to build rapport and shows respect.

There are more techniques on dealing with difficult and angry customers in chapter 16, but a positive inner voice is the first step to handling this successfully.

You can't win everyone over but you can deal with them in a professional manner. Everyone has a point of view and it doesn't have to be the same as yours. In fact life would be pretty boring if it was. We are all individual personalities, with different upbringing and experiences, which influence the way we communicate.

Keep an open mind and seek first to understand and then be understood and you won't go far wrong.

QUICK RECAP

- *There are three main types of behaviour: assertive, aggressive and submissive.*
- *Submissive means neglecting to defend your personal rights and beliefs.*
- *Aggressive means considering your rights and beliefs are more important than other people's.*
- *Assertive means standing up for your own rights without violating the rights of others.*
- *Being assertive means that you are confident enough to express your opinions, views and ideas and to deal with customers in a professional manner.*
- *People behave aggressively because it gives them a sense of power and sometimes it covers up for their own insecurity; people also behave aggressively if they are threatened.*
- *People become submissive when they are under attack or when they think they are going to be attacked.*
- *Submissive individuals usually have low self-esteem.*
- *To build assertiveness focus on your positive points, and your strengths. Tell yourself these, keep your body language open and make sure you have a positive inner voice.*

CHAPTER 15

Getting on the customer's wavelength

I mentioned at the beginning of this book that it is not simply a case of understanding a group of customers needs but also understanding an *individual* customer's needs. Therefore, in order to deliver exceptional customer service the employee dealing directly with the customer must get on that customer's wavelength, just as the good manager must get on the employee's wavelength in order to understand how to motivate him. This chapter examines the different personalities and how by understanding them and responding appropriately the employee can deliver the ultimate in customer service.

HOW TO WIN OVER THE CUSTOMER

The more you have in common with someone the easier it is to get along with them.

We are more easily influenced by those we like hence the saying, 'people buy people', as any sales person worth his salt should know. If we like someone we are more inclined to buy from them and to co-operate with them.

Conflict usually results from differences or perceived differences between people. So enhancing this likeability factor can reduce conflict. The more you blend with the other person the more they will be satisfied with the service you are providing.

Mirror body language

You can do this by mirroring their body language. I don't mean mimicking it but gently matching it. For example if the customer leans forward then you should gently lean forward to show interest and build rapport. If the customer moves back from you then move back too. When we get on well with someone we naturally mirror body language.

ACTION POINT

Watch people in a café, restaurant or at a bar and see how similar their body language is. If they are mirroring each other then they are getting on fine. If they are keeping their distance and have different body language then the rapport isn't there. You can also see this in television programmes where one member of a panel on a quiz programme will pick up a glass of water and drink from it, so too will some of the others on his team.

Understanding personalities

Everyone is different. You think you are 'normal' but what is normal? Normal is different to each and every one of us. We see the world through our own eyes, we think everyone should behave, act and be like us. Well, of course they don't. We are all different. We all have different personalities. Understanding this and recognising this can help you adapt your approach to another person and get on their wavelength.

In 1926 William Marston came up with a model of Personality Types that is still used today. Whilst people are highly complex and certainly more complex than the descriptions I am going to give you, this model will, I hope, help you to see yourself and others in a different light, and, so by seeing this, enable you to change tactics to communicate more effectively, and build better rapport with your customers.

We inherit personality traits from our parents, grandparents, great grandparents and so on. Of course this is influenced by other factors like upbringing, environment, education and levels of intellect and maturity but to make things simpler I will look at the four basic types of personalities. Although we may contain a mixture of these traits some will be stronger than others within us. This dictates how we communicate and behave. See if you can recognise yourself from the descriptions below. Then think about how you might need to change your approach towards a customer in order to build better rapport with them and deliver the ultimate in customer service.

Type A – Dominant personalities

Type A personalities have dominance and superiority in their make up. This makes them rather impatient individuals. They are very direct people who 'speak as they find' and 'don't suffer fools gladly'. They are confident decision makers (although these may not always be the right decisions) but there is no pussy-footing around with these types. They are extremely time conscious and find it hard to relax. They are always doing something and even on holiday, if they take one, will want to be using the time 'wisely'. They can be rather intolerant of others who are slower than them. They are the type of customers who will have no difficulty in complaining, and will want a very quick and efficient service with high and exacting standards. Their body language will often be very positive and can sometimes be overpowering as can be their manner of speaking. You might find them rather abrupt, and if speaking to them on the telephone could think them rude, but this might not necessarily be so. It is just their manner.

TOP TIPS

Your best response to highly dominant, quick speaking people is to adopt a businesslike manner, be crisp and efficient, but obviously not unfriendly.

Speed up the way you talk, be direct, get straight to the point and ensure that your handshake is firm and your body language positive.

Don't go into too much detail. For example, don't go through the minute details of a service or product or they will quickly get bored and irritated and cut you short.

Be clear, specific, brief and to the point.

> Make this customer feel special by making him feel *very* important.

Type B – Social personalities

The Type B is a 'people-person' and likes to be liked. They find it much easier than any of the other personality types to mirror and match another person's body language because they are more attuned to people's needs and moods. This means they are usually very good in a customer service role. They are adaptable, flexible and participative. They have high energy levels and are articulate, confident and co-operative. They are enthusiastic, embracing and thrive on change. Their body language will be open and positive.

They are usually highly persuasive individuals but find it hard to deal with confrontation. They will complain but in a much more friendly style than our dominant personality. They will be friendly, talkative and smiling at you. Indeed you may have trouble shutting them up! They won't be as direct and forthright as the Type A dominant personality.

TOP TIPS

Spend more time over the pleasantries, take time to get to know them.

Be friendly.

Use positive open body language including maintaining good eye contact.

This type of customer will want to take time to get to know you and your organisation. They will be demanding but not in the same way as the dominant individual.

> Make this customer feel special by forging a good relationship with them.

If you do so then this customer will not only be loyal but will be highly influential in recommending you to others.

Type C – Measured personalities

The Type C is a measured personality in that they are far more logical and analytical than either our A (dominant) or our B (social) personality. They are steady, often security minded and don't like a lot of change. They can be suspicious and sceptical of new ideas and it will take some time to persuade them.

They are consistent, caring and patient. They don't like taking risks and will only do so if they have weighed up all the pro's and con's. They are great list makers!

Their body language is more closed and they can be looking at you rather sceptically. They will sit well back in their chair with their arms folded, not necessarily with hostility, but they will reserve judgment on you and what you are saying until they have weighed you up and decided whether or not they like you.

They are often silent, and can be difficult to draw out. You will need to use 'open' questions to get them to talk and to provide you with the information you need. The Type C personality is also often slower speaking. If you are an A (dominant) or B (social) personality you could find this rather frustrating, and will need to curb your desire to jump in and answer your own questions, or finish off their sentences for them.

This is the type of customer who will require all the details from you. You will need to patiently explain the product or service benefits and go through applications and procedures carefully and painstakingly. If you don't slow down and provide this customer with what he wants he certainly won't buy from you, and will never return.

Because of their cautious nature Type C's can have a tendency to procrastinate and over-plan. They are generally warm hearted but when aggressive can be very stubborn and intransient. So if they have a complaint to make they will certainly dig their heels in. Their influencing style is based on logic and facts and you will need to have these to hand. Fairness is also paramount to a Type C personality.

> Make this customer feel special by listening to him without interrupting. Take time to break the ice and make yourself agreeable.

TOP TIPS

Be sincere and show a genuine interest in them.
Take time to find areas of common ground.
Be honest and open and patiently draw them out in a non-threatening manner.
Slow down, move casually and informally.
Provide lots of assurances and give clear specific solutions with maximum guarantees.
Give them the detail. If you don't, they will ask for it.
You can't fob them off. Don't rush them.
Do not patronise or show irritation.

Once you have gained the confidence and trust of this type of personality they are often extremely loyal.

Type D – Compliant personalities

The Type D personality likes to comply with the rules and regulations. This means that they are usually very systematic, precise, hyper-efficient and bureaucratic. These people love facts and detail, the more the better, and even more than our Type C.

They can often be shy and self-effacing with closed and hunched body language. You will often get lowered eye contact and fidgeting mannerisms. There will be no dominant body language. The handshake can be perfunctory and not terribly firm. They will speak quietly and can be vague.

Their compliant nature means they can often be easily agreeing which makes it difficult for you to know exactly what they are really feeling and thinking. They need to feel completely sure of their position and of others' expectations. They can give the impression of coldness and lack of interest and will use rules, authority and logical argument to influence the actions of others. They have a tendency to correct errors and inaccuracies that others might consider insignificant so you might find them irritating if your personality errs towards the A (dominant) or B (social). If you let this show then you will lose a customer.

This customer is a lot less likely to complain but when they do they will be rigid and nit-picking. They are concerned with quality, and do not want to accept inferior work regardless of timescales so make sure you get it right. They are punctual and like punctuality in others so if you turn up a few minutes late you could find you've lost the business before you've even had a chance to win it.

TOP TIPS

Be straightforward in your approach, stick to the business in hand, don't digress into social chit chat – they don't want it.
Build credibility by listing the pros and cons to any suggestions you make.
Reassure them that there won't be any surprises.
Be realistic and accurate and provide solid, tangible, practical evidence like testimonials.
Give them time to make any decisions.

Make this customer feel special by allowing them plenty of time to make up their mind but at the same time gently directing them.

There are, of course, many more complexities of personalities than I have given you here, but I hope the above goes some way in helping you to understand that we are all different and because of this we need to accept that different approaches work with different people. Being aware of the different personalities, reading the body language and keeping an open mind so that you try and understand where the other person is coming from can all combine to help you relate to your customers (and staff) more effectively.

QUICK RECAP

- *The more you have in common with someone the easier it is to get along with them.*
- *'People buy people' so enhancing the likeability factor can help us to influence others.*
- *We are all different; understanding and recognising different personalities can help us to adapt our approach and hence improve customer relationships.*

CHAPTER 16

Dealing with the angry or difficult person

Dealing with angry people is never easy. Anger can come at us out of the blue when we least expect it and catch us unawares. It can leave us (and the customer) feeling very upset and frustrated. You need to learn how to express yourself without losing your temper or bursting into tears. This chapter will provide you with some techniques to help you deal with anger in an effective way and stay assertive.

THE STAGES OF ANGER

In order to deal with an angry customer you need to understand that there are three stages of anger which a person can go through, and these escalate at each stage if the anger is not handled professionally and effectively at the first critical stage.

Stage One

When someone is very angry they usually approach you ranting and raving, or they are shouting at you down the phone.

> People are usually braver on the telephone when complaining than they are face-to-face because the visual element is missing so the anger may be more intense.

This can obviously be very upsetting because it feels like a personal onslaught. It isn't. And it is very important that you tell yourself this.

So make sure you get the right positive inner voice from the start. Tell yourself that you can handle this, you can deal with it, even if at this stage you are quaking in your shoes. If your brain is telling your body that it can deal with it this will send positive messages to your body language and not only will you feel more able to handle the situation but you will also start projecting positive body language.

Next, tell yourself that the customer isn't angry with you, personally, but at something that your organisation has done (albeit possibly by a member of staff) to annoy that customer.

> The customer is angry at the situation, not you.

Perhaps your organisation has failed to deliver what was promised. Perhaps someone has sent the customer the wrong piece of equipment. Maybe a promised call back hasn't materialised. Whatever the reason, your task is to try and resolve the problem.

If you don't successfully resolve the anger at Stage One then it will escalate to Stage Two. I examine techniques to help you handle all these stages of anger later in this chapter.

Stage Two

Now the anger intensifies and becomes directed at you personally. This is where you may get abusive language and threats.

Stage Three

The third level of anger is where it becomes directed at everyone else. This may not sound very harmful, but believe me it could ruin your organisation's reputation.

At this stage of anger the customer is threatening to call the newspapers, contact a consumer affairs programme, take your organisation to court, and generally tell everyone how useless your company is. They could write about you on their blog, put negative comments on review websites and spread the word about you through the internet to hundreds and thousands of potential customers. Bad news travels fast and your sales could be seriously affected.

> Anger needs to be resolved at Stage One when it is directed at the situation and not you personally.

UNDERSTANDING WHY PEOPLE USE ANGER

Believe it or not many people find it very difficult to complain. Some would rather not say anything but just slide away and never use your company's services or products again. This is bad news because you never then have a chance to put things right. And of course, as I've already mentioned, these people will tell others how dreadful your company is. You *want* customers to complain *to you* if something has gone wrong.

If someone is going to complain they often have to work

themselves up into a head of steam to do so. Before facing you they could be feeling nervous because they fear you won't understand what they are saying, or they are preparing themselves to be met by resistance and disbelief. Some people lack the vocabulary to express their true feelings and are afraid that they will be ridiculed. This means that by the time they call you on the telephone, or come storming into your office or shop, they are ready to let rip. So, how do you deal with angry customers?

10 steps to handling the angry customer

Step 1. Get the right inner voice

Tell yourself that you can handle this; you can keep calm. The customer is not angry at you but at something that has happened. You need to resolve this to your and the customer's satisfaction.

Some positive inner voice phrases

'I can handle this.'

'I can keep calm.'

'This is not directed at me personally.'

'I need to help the customer resolve this.'

Step 2. Get the right body language

If you are face-to-face with the customer then keep your body posture upright, but not stiff or aggressive, and hold eye contact as best you can. Some people won't look at you when they are very angry; instead their eye contact is roving all over the place. Alternatively, some angry people may be glaring at you and it can be very intimidating holding their eye contact.

The moment you drop eye contact you have behaved submissively and this gives the customer the chance to walk all over you. Alternatively if your eyes are above or beyond the customer, refusing to look at him, coupled with a slouched posture this is communicating a 'couldn't care less' attitude and is guaranteed to send the customer's temper soaring even further.

Step 3. Listen actively

Don't let your mind get distracted by thinking negative thoughts about the other person. If you're thinking, 'This customer is a pain' or 'How dare he talk to me like that!' this will show in your body language and you won't really be listening – critically listening.

Make listening noises to show that you are listening, particularly on the telephone. If face-to-face then occasionally nod to show you are listening.

Step 4. Do not try to interrupt the customer or reason with him

> You can never begin to reason with someone until they have worked their anger out.

Let the customer get it off their chest. They need to have their say. Eventually they will run out of steam. They will have to pause if only to take a breath. It is only after this that you can move on to the next stage. If you need to isolate the customer from the public area then trying to do so whilst they are in full flow is disastrous. It will only fuel their anger, as will interrupting them and trying to reason with them. Unfortunately if someone does erupt in a public area, you just have to adopt the above techniques and put up with it. It is not pleasant but it *will* pass if handled correctly, and you *will* be able to resolve whatever is upsetting the customer.

Step 5. Restate/summarise the situation

Now that the customer has had his say you have the opportunity to speak. Here you need to sum up what the customer has told you. For example, *'Let me check I've understood, Mr. Jones. We promised you delivery of this equipment on Tuesday and you've still not received it, is that correct?'* The customer now knows that you have listened and understood the situation correctly. If you have misunderstood, this allows the customer the opportunity of correcting you. If you can use the customer's name in conversation this also helps you to build rapport.

Step 6. Ask open questions.

If you are not in a position to summarise from what the customer has said, because you need more information, then you may need to ask **open questions** to probe deeper, to find out exactly what is the problem. Alternatively you may need to ask further **questions** to correctly resolve the problem. Here is a reminder of what open questions begin with:

- **Who**
- **What**
- **Where**
- **When**
- **How**
- **Why**

For example:
'When did we promise you delivery, Mr Brown?'
'Who did you speak to about this?'
'How many items did you receive?'

There are further types of questions that could help you handle the awkward or difficult situation. Here are some of them.

Exploratory questions, which are also open questions
'What happened after that?'
'What do you mean by that?'

Clarifying the situation and summarising
'Let me just make sure I've understood this, Mr Smith. What you're saying is...'
'I'm not sure I understand, Mrs Jones, could you clarify that for me please?'

Interpreting
'Are you perhaps saying…?'

Supportive
'Do please go on.' Encouraging the customer and reassuring him.

Empathic
'It sounds as though…'
'I can see that you're obviously very upset about this.'
'I understand, Mr Jones, and I would be angry with that if it happened to me. Now let me see how I can resolve this for you.'

Reflective
Repeating statements made in a reflective way.

Self-disclosing
This is where you can share your own experiences about a particular issue. For example: 'That happened to me once and I completely understand how you must feel. Now let me see how I can resolve this for you.'

It is at this stage that you may wish to isolate the customer from the public area. After restating the problem you might wish to say something along the lines of: 'Let's take a seat in the interview room, Mr. Jones, and then I can resolve this situation for you.'

By now the customer's anger will hopefully have subsided and he will be ready to answer your questions and accompany you to a private area.

Beneficial intent Statement

In the example above I have used what is called the **beneficial intent statement** –'Let's take a seat in the interview room, Mr. Jones and let me see **how I can resolve this situation for you**.'

> The beneficial intent statement strengthens the bond between you and the customer.

Step 7. Resolve it

Now you need to tell the customer how you are going to resolve the situation for him, ie what you are going to do about his complaint.

Another very effective technique is to ask the customer what he would like you to do, thereby putting the ball in his court. For example, 'How might I resolve this for you, Mr Smith?' Or 'What would you like me to do, Mr Smith?'

Step 8. Then do it

Take action. Don't promise to resolve something and then do nothing about it.

Step 9. Follow up

Check that any action promised has been carried out even if it wasn't your responsibility to do so. If you took the complaint, you must take responsibility for seeing it through to a satisfactory conclusion.

As a final gesture telephone the customer and check that the situation has been resolved to his satisfaction. This final touch often turns what was a potentially disastrous customer relations exercise into a good one, and you may have won a customer for life if handled professionally and efficiently.

Step 10. Then ask, what would have prevented this problem?

What changes do you need to make to ensure it doesn't happen again? An organisation that continually allows mistakes to happen and doesn't deliver its promises isn't going to be around for very long.

Additional points on taking angry calls

Follow the same steps as previously described. If you have taken an angry telephone call, and need to ask the customer to wait whilst you check something, then be lavish in explaining what you are doing, especially if it involves a silence while the caller 'hangs on'. Remember he can't see you, and he will interpret any silence as inactivity. If you need to put the customer on hold then assure him that you will get back to him promptly, or offer to ring him back, and tell him when that will be. Don't say, 'I'll call you back later.' This is too vague. Later to you might mean tomorrow morning when the customer is expecting a call within the next 30 minutes. If the customer has to call your organisation again, he will be VERY ANGRY, especially if he has to explain the problem all over again, and to someone else.

Take ownership of the problem. For example say 'I will call you back in 20 minutes' and *then do so*, even if you are still trying to track down an answer. Telling the customer that you are still 'on the case' will make him much happier.

This kind of follow up can often be difficult for some organisations that operate call centres where staff are working on different shifts. It is often one of the reasons why call centres get a bad press. It is no excuse. A call centre must find ways of operating in an efficient manner by putting the customer's needs first. After all no customers no organisation!

How to handle difficult/angry customers

DON'T

- Interrupt
- Be patronising
- Jump to conclusions
- Argue
- Lose your temper
- Blame others

DO

- Be quiet and listen
- Use the customer's name
- Take notes – but not too many if face-to-face, remember to keep that eye contact
- Let the customer make his case
- Ask questions to clarify the details
- Confirm with the customer that you understand the nature of the problem
- Tell the customer what you propose to do to put things right
- Make sure it is done
- Show empathy

HANDLING THE UNREASONABLE AND AGGRESSIVE CUSTOMER

Now let's take this a step further. What if the customer *isn't* right? Their grievance may be unjustified, or perhaps despite everything they won't calm down or be reasonable, what happens then? Here you need to adopt what is called the **consequence technique.**

The Consequence Technique

You should follow steps 1 to 5 as discussed in the previous section on dealing with the difficult customer:

1. Get the right inner voice
2. Get the right body language
3. Listen actively
4. Don't interrupt or try to reason with them – let the customer have his head of steam
5. Restate/summarise the situation

You may even get to the next stage and be able to ask some open questions to try and find out what is at the root of the problem. Or you may need to explain your company's procedure or policy that puts the customer in the wrong and you in the right. In this case you need to follow these steps:

1. **State where you stand but show you are still interested in the customer's opinions and feelings**
   For example: *'I recognise you have strong feelings on this, Mrs. Smith, but we see it differently.'*
   Here you have also empathised to a degree by recognising the customer's feelings but you have balanced this with stating your viewpoint. You may need to continue by adding something along the lines of: *'It is our policy not to allow smoking, (dogs) (children) because…'* and give a valid reason.
   If the aggression is still maintained then you need to:
2. **Step up your assertiveness. Increase the emphasis on your position.**
   For example: *'It is our policy.'*
   If the aggression continues and the customer becomes abusive then:
3. Use the **consequence technique**.
   For example: *'If you continue to shout in this way, Mrs Smith, I will put the phone down and ring you back later when you have calmed down'* or *'If you continue to behave in this manner, Mrs Smith, then I must ask you to leave.'*

If all your efforts have failed then cut off the interaction, as you have warned them.

EXAMPLE

I was working in a busy inner city job centre. A customer became very abusive towards me. I warned him that if he continued to shout and swear at me I would refuse to deal with him. When he didn't stop I got up from my desk and walked away. I had a great boss who backed me up and told the man that until he learnt how to behave no one would deal with him.

TOP TIPS

Whatever the reason for the anger try to keep calm, get a positive inner voice and hold on to it. Try first to understand how the other person feels, where they are coming from, rather than focusing on how you feel.

WORDS AND PHRASES TO AVOID

There are some words and phrases that really annoy customers. Here are some of the more common ones:

Problem

If the customer is angry and you say to him or her 'What's the problem?' or even worse, 'What's your problem,' they are likely to reply, 'I haven't got a problem – it's your company that's got the problem.' Try and avoid this word as much as you can. Rephrase it if possible to: 'How can I help you?' Or 'Explain to me what happened?'

Complaint

Likewise the word 'complaint' invites people to make a complaint and also sounds as if they've got something wrong with them medically. Why not simply say, 'Please tell me what happened?' or 'What's the situation?'

You have to

A very emotive phrase particularly if the customer is angry. He may well say, 'I don't *have* to do anything.' Instead you could say, 'Could I ask you to put that in writing, Mr. Jones?'

You must appreciate

This often sends customers screaming up the wall! The customer could retaliate by saying, 'I don't have to appreciate anything, particularly when it is done to suit your organisation and not me, the customer!' 'Why must I appreciate your problems? I am the customer. I am paying for this service or product.' The customer doesn't have to appreciate the way you run your organisation – he is only concerned with what has inconvenienced him.

There's nothing I can do.

Always tell people what you **can** do – not what you can't do. Or simply say, 'Let me check on that and get back to you.' And, don't forget, always tell them when you will get back to them.

He's out at the moment

By all means say if someone isn't available but then ask if anyone else can help, or if you can take a message. The number of times I have had to ask whether anyone else can help me is incredible. Always volunteer that extra bit of information or help.

TOP TIPS

Try to use 'I apologise', it sounds more assertive than 'I'm sorry'.

It is never very pleasant dealing with an angry customer but most people get angry for a reason, and that is because your organisation, or someone in it, has done or not done something to make them angry. If you adopt the above techniques you can usually resolve the situation to the customer's satisfaction and yours. It is vital that customer facing staff have adequate training in handling difficult customers and that there is a procedure in place to deal with and support those staff who might have to handle abusive and aggressive customers.

AGGRESSION AND CONFLICT FROM A WORK COLLEAGUE

Aggression and conflict doesn't only come from customers; you could also find yourself in conflict with a colleague. This in turn can affect your performance and therefore your ability to deal with your customers. Conflict at work can arise for all sorts of reasons, and should be managed constructively to the benefit of everyone concerned.

Typical areas of conflict include:

- Mediating between two colleagues.
- A colleague who wants the same resources as you but thinks his need is greater.
- Handling crises and unforeseen events in the workplace.

Handling Conflict

Make sure you stay assertive. Get a positive inner dialogue. Don't go on the defensive and argue back, instead ask yourself why this person is behaving in this manner. Sometimes there is no logical reason, but keep calm and deal with them in a professional manner. Conflict often results from differences or perceived differences – try and understand the other person's viewpoint, and make sure you have a positive inner voice. Blending with the other person can maximise similarities and minimise conflict. Use body language to enhance this; mirror their physical stance, match their voice in volume and speed of conversation.

ACTION POINT

Reflect on typical reactions to conflict situations and ask yourself:

- When do I avoid conflict?
- When do I accommodate others?
- How often do I secure a compromise?
- When do I compete strongly with others?
- Which situations cause me to be bitter and resentful afterwards?
- What alternatives are there for handling situations better?

If you get upset, try to remove yourself from the environment. Excuse yourself to go to the toilet or to return an urgent telephone call. Get a positive inner voice; tell yourself you can deal with it. Calm yourself down before going back and resolving conflict. And reward yourself every time you deal with a potentially awkward situation in a positive manner even if it is just giving yourself a pat on the back.

QUICK RECAP

- *Aggressive people can come at us out of the blue when we are least prepared for them.*
- *There are three stages of anger:*
  - *Stage One: The customer is angry at the situation, not you.*
  - *Stage Two: The anger becomes directed at you personally.*
  - *Stage Three: The customer is threatening to sue you or tell the world how bad you are.*
- *Anger needs to be resolved at Stage One when it is directed at the situation.*
- *By the time people complain they have usually worked themselves up into a state.*
- *Ask what would have prevented this problem? What changes do we need to make to ensure it doesn't happen again?*
- *If the customer's grievance is unjustified step up your assertiveness and if he becomes abusive, or refuses to calm down, adopt the consequence technique.*
- *Whatever the reason for anger do try to keep calm, adopt a positive inner voice and hold on to it.*
- *Try first to understand how the other person feels, where* ***they*** *are coming from, rather than focusing on how* ***you*** *feel.*

CHAPTER 17

Steps to exceptional service

AND FINALLY…

It's not just about meeting your customers' expectations but about exceeding them. By doing this you can win more business. Here are some further tips on how you can do this:

Take time to communicate with your customers on a regular basis in the manner that they prefer. This could be by email, telephone, letter, newsletter, in person, and in some businesses by inviting them to a corporate hospitality event.

Ask them how they prefer to be contacted and then contact them using their preferred method. Also check the frequency of contact: some may need or like fairly regular contact, others might find this too overwhelming.

Collect information on your customers and their buying habits and patterns and use this to communicate with them in the most effective way, tailoring promotional offers to suit them, or providing them with new information about products or services.

Make sure that your website design reflects your customer base and is easy to navigate and packed with the right information. Make it easy for your customers to find what they need on your website quickly. In addition, make it simple for your customers to contact you by the most appropriate methods for your organisation. If they are responding or enquiring via your website ensure that you capture this information and, with their permission, use it to correspond with them regularly.

Telephone or survey your customers on a regular basis to check they are happy with your products and services and introduce new services and products if appropriate.

If appropriate to your business ensure you have the right account managers calling on your existing customers and checking they are satisfied with your organisation's services. Don't let them just be order takers. Their job is to sell more to your customers by offering them solutions to their problems, or by satisfying a need.

Undertake marketing initiatives that benefit your local community, for example become involved in charitable donations or fundraising events. This not only raises your profile but communicates a caring message.

Your staff may wish to work with voluntary organisations, or on projects in the community. This not only helps develop them as individuals but also enriches the local community. Getting a group of staff to work on a charitable project in the community is also a great team building exercise.

Look at operating environmentally and eco friendly policies.

And finally… **Take care of your staff and they will take care of your customers.**

CHAPTER 18

Quickstart guide: summary of key points

Chapter 1 Why good customer service is essential

- If you don't look after your customers then someone else will.
- Dissatisfied customers will tell others about their awful experience with you.
- Once you have a negative reputation it is extremely difficult to reverse it.
- Providing good customer service is essential for the survival and success of your business.
- Delivering exceptional customer service can reap rewards in terms of job satisfaction, motivated staff and increased profits.
- Satisfied customers become advocates and repeat purchasers, and recommend you to others.
- Excellent customer service can give you an edge on your competitors.
- You and your staff need to develop good interpersonal skills.
- You need to put in place a good customer service policy.

Chapter 2 Knowing your customers

- Different groups of customers have different needs, and individuals within the groups will also have different requirements.
- The more you know about your customers the more successful you will be in delivering to them the kind of exceptional service/products they require.
- Suppliers and staff form an impression of the organisation and that impression is communicated to the outside world – make sure it isn't a negative one.
- When people buy a product or service they also consider the emotional factors that surround that purchase.
- By understanding and delivering these emotional factors to your customers, and satisfying them consistently, you will excel in providing customer service and gain a competitive advantage.

- People generally buy for two reasons: objective and subjective reasons, and in order, to deliver good customer service you will need to satisfy both of these.
- Customer Relationship Management software can help you capture the information you need to identify who your customers are and categorise their behaviour.
- You might also be able to get this information from conducting customer surveys or by analysing your existing database, or by analysing the buying patterns of your website visitors.

Chapter 3 Your customer service philosophy

- Having a clearly defined image of what your organisation stands for, consistently communicating it and living up to that image is what it takes to stand out from the crowd.
- Staff need to be involved in developing this image and in writing a customer service orientated mission statement to sum this up.
- You never get a second chance to make a first impression and neither does your organisation.
- First impressions are often lasting impressions and could lose you vital business if they are negative.
- Take a long, hard look at your organisation from the prospective customer's viewpoint: is it giving out the right impression?
- Are the staff giving out the right impression?
- Ask your customers, staff and other visitors for their views.
- Make sure your front line staff are fully trained and able and willing to deal with the customer effectively and efficiently.
- Ensure you have a policy that says how the telephone should be answered and how calls should be handled.
- Ensure you have a policy that states how customer complaints should be handled.
- If an organisation doesn't care for the workplace environment and the well-being of its staff, then the staff won't care for the organisation.

- Be consistent in your messages both inside and outside the organisation.

Chapter 4 Setting standards

- In order to prevent misunderstandings between staff and management, and between individuals, develop a set of standards on how you expect staff to behave towards customers.
- Standards can also encompass how you wish the services you provide to customers to be delivered, or the acceptable level of quality of the products you manufacture.

  The more common standards are:

  – Behaviour

  – Dress/appearance

  –Delivery of your service

  – Quality of your product

  – Environmental

  – Customers complaints
- In order to avoid dissent you need to involve your staff in drawing up these standards.
- Make it clear to staff what is expected of them and give them a real sense of personal responsibility.
- Each process or procedure that is carried out needs to be examined to ensure that it matches the customer's experience of your organisation, and the customer's satisfaction with your products or service.
- Examine what you need to do, if anything, to improve customer satisfaction.
- Adhere to those standards yourself and encourage your staff to contribute new ideas/better ways of doing things.

Chapter 5 Improving communication

- Most problems within organisations boil down to two things: weak management and poor communication.

- Communication involves actively inviting opionions, talking to individuals fact-to-face and listening to them.
- Staff need to feel they are simultaneously informed, involved and sharing in the success of the organisation.
- Encourage your staff to contribute new ideas and suggest better ways of doing things.
- The benefits to be gained from improving communication include better delivery of customer service, more focused staff, better profitability.
- Communication is not telling – it is involving. It has to come from the bottom up as well as the top down.
- Make sure you have a system to capture ideas and to explore and discuss them.

Chapter 6 Motivating your staff

- Motivating your staff is a vital part of providing exceptional customer service.
- Good customer service demands good managers.
- The good manager/director will have an acute awareness that people matter and an understanding of the many human characteristics which can inhibit progress.
- To get the best out of your staff you will need persistence and patience accompanied by a willingness to adapt or alter direction when required.
- The effective manager/director will embrace change, have enthusiasm for the training and development of his staff, be prepared to face problems and deal with them, and know how obstacles can be overcome.
- Motivation is encouraging, inspiring, influencing and stimulating people to perform well.
- Happy staff make happy customers which menus increased sales and profits.
- People come to work for a variety of reasons, and understanding why individuals within your team or organisation come to

work can be one of the first steps to finding out what motivates them.

- In order to feel involved and motivated staff need to have a group pride, ie pride in their team and/or organisation.
- Give the individual as much control over the work they do as you can, don't keep checking up on them.
- Make sure you give your staff clear direction and that they know and understand what is expected of them.
- Communication plays a considerable part in helping to motivate staff to perform well.

Chapter 7 Training and development

- Provide ongoing training to ensure you have knowledgeable and confident staff.
- Training is both a motivator and a means of communication. It can be job or product specific, or include training in interpersonal skills, core customer skills, team building, problem solving, developing creativity, leadership, management, or in something completely unrelated to the workplace.
- Training must help develop the individual to achieve his or her objectives and hence contribute towards achieving the organisation's objectives.
- There are many different ways that training can be delivered and which method you use depends on the objectives for training, the employee, and the type and availability of training.
- Be aware of the different attitudes towards training. Whilst some may welcome it and see it as a reward others will see it as a form of punishment.
- You need to plan for training to be successful, set and agree objectives and evaluate the training provided.
- Coaching is another form of ongoing staff development and can be used alongside training or as an alternative to it.
- In order to conduct good coaching practices you need to create a partnership with the person you are coaching.

- The coaching session should be a completely separate meeting between the two people concerned.
- Agree the topic for coaching and ensure that longer term goals are achievable, timed and measurable. Also agree goals for each session at the outset.

Chapter 8 Measure, monitor and reward

- You can monitor staff performance by giving regular staff appraisals.
- The appraisal is intended to help staff achieve their full potential and build towards providing a quality service.
- Shared ideas and views lead to better customer service and a more motivated workforce.
- A performance appraisal is a review of the employee's skills and knowledge related to the job.
- Appraisals should be given yearly. You should always give the staff member time to prepare for them and you should thoroughly prepare yourself.
- Employees who feel valued will give better service.
- You can reward staff by giving praise, by involving them in decision making, and by seeking their opinions and listening to them.

Chapter 9 Customer surveys

- Nothing stays the same – your customers' views will change and so too will their needs and wants.
- Keep in touch with your customers and their views by regularly surveying them.
- When wording a survey you need to ensure that you get unbiased answers – ask 'open' questions.
- Be clear from the outset what you wish to achieve from the customer satisfaction survey.

- The easy questions should be at the beginning of the survey. The more complex and those requiring a comment answer towards the end of the survey.
- Act on the survey results – examine those areas where customers have been critical, and look at how you can improve things.
- Providing excellent customer service starts with recruiting the right staff.

Chapter 10 Voice and telephone handling techniques

- 93% of the impression you give out is based on your voice.
- If you work on the telephone, handling customer queries and complaints, then how you sound is vitally important.
- Subtleties of voice are far greater than we think. We can read an enormous amount into the vocal tone of people on the telephone in the first few seconds.
- It's not what you say it's the way that you say it! Enthusiasm is infectious; inject it in your voice.
- Lower the pitch of your voice and slow down when you speak to make each word sound clearer.
- Keeping your body language still will also inject more authority into your voice.
- Vary the pitch and pace of your voice to sound interesting and enthusiastic.
- Practise projecting your voice and avoid using fillers such as 'you know'.
- Try not to finish your sentences on a high as if you are asking a question when you are actually stating a fact as it will weaken what you are saying.
- Record your voice in order to become aware of how much or how little energy you transmit to others.
- Good telephone practice includes answering the telephone promptly, apologising for keeping the caller waiting,

announcing who you are, and establishing and using the other person's name early in the telephone conversation.

- Smile – even though you can't be seen by the other person, if you smile it helps your voice to sound more assertive and friendly.
- Mirror/pace your voice with the customer. Vary your pitch and make sure you do not sound dull.

Chapter 11 Appearance and body language

- Staff who deal with customers give out an impression of your organisation. How you look plays an important part in creating an impression.
- How you project yourself through your body language is vitally important.
- Non-verbal signals are said to be at least four and a half times as effective as verbal signals, and facial expressions are eight times as powerful as the words used.
- We look at someone a third of the time we are talking to them and this look can convey anything from boredom and irritation to enthusiasm and liking.
- You can enhance the image you project and your feelings of self-confidence by deliberately using more positive body language.
- Your handshake can say a great deal about you. A firm, dry handshake reveals confidence, professionalism and status.
- Personal space is the space around us that we feel comfortable with; don't threaten others by invading their personal space.
- Keep your posture upright, your shoulders back and your chin up.
- Eye contact and a smile are important parts of welcoming customers and showing you are interested.

Chapter 12 Listening

- Listening is an essential part of being a good communicator and therefore essential to customer service.
- Listening involves:
  - the ability to understand what is being said
  - the ability to organise and analyse the messages in order to retain them for subsequent use.
- There are two types of listening: casual listening and critical listening.
- There are many reasons why we don't listen properly: physical tiredness or discomfort, desire to talk, different perspectives, strong emotions and prejudices, preconceived ideas, reactions to the speaker, simple distractions and our mind wandering.

Chapter 13 Questioning and interpreting needs

- In addition to listening to the customer you also need to be able to interpret their needs accurately. In order to do this you will need to ask the correct questions.
- Open questions are those that require an answer other than simply a 'yes' or 'no'. They begin with, 'What', 'Where', 'When', 'How', 'Why' and 'Who'.
- Closed questions usually elicit a single word response, 'yes' or 'no'. They begin with: 'Is/Are', 'Should/Shall', 'Can/Could', 'Will/Would', 'Do/Did'.
- Both sorts of questions are needed to elicit different types of information, enabling you to deliver service that meets your customer's needs.

Chapter 14 Assertiveness

- There are three main types of behaviour: assertive, aggressive and submissive.
- Submissive means neglecting to defend your personal rights and beliefs.

- Aggressive means considering your rights and beliefs are more important than other people's.
- Assertive means standing up for your own rights without violating the rights of others.
- Being assertive means that you are confident enough to express your opinions, views and ideas and to deal with customers in a professional manner.
- People behave aggressively because it gives them a sense of power and sometimes it covers up for their own insecurity.
- People also behave aggressively if they are threatened.
- People become submissive when they are under attack or when they think they are going to be attacked.
- Submissive individuals usually have low self-esteem.
- To build assertiveness focus on your positive points, and your strengths. Tell yourself these, keep your body language open and make sure you have a positive inner voice.

Chapter 15 Getting on the customer's wavelength

- The more you have in common with someone the easier it is to get along with them.
- 'People buy people' so enhancing the likeability factor can help us to influence others.
- We are all different; understanding and recognising different personalities can help us to adapt our approach and hence improve customer relationships.

Chapter 16 Dealing with the angry or difficult person

- Aggressive people can come at us out of the blue when we are least prepared for them.
- There are three stages of anger:
  - Stage One: – The customer is angry at the situation, not you
  - Stage Two: – The anger becomes directed at you personally

- Stage Three: – The customer is threatening to sue you and tell the world how bad you are

- Anger needs to be resolved at Stage One when it is directed at the situation and not you personally.
- By the time people complain they have usually worked themselves up into a state.
- Ask what would have prevented this problem? What changes do we need to make to ensure it doesn't happen again?
- If the customer's grievance is unjustified step up your assertiveness and if he becomes abusive, or refuses to calm down, adopt the consequence technique.
- Whatever the reason for anger do try to keep calm, adopt a positive inner voice and hold on to it.
- Try first to understand how the other person feels, where *they* are coming from, rather than focusing on how *you* feel.

CHAPTER 19

Troubleshooting

Question: Just lately we seem to be losing some of our most regular and long-standing customers and can't understand why. What should we do?

Firstly do you know where these customers are going instead of coming to you? Could a competitor have recently started up, and if so are they offering any special promotions that are attracting your customers?

If the customers you are losing have been loyal for some time then it usually takes a lot for them to deflect to the competition, so you need to examine what your organisation might be doing wrong to cause them to deflect. Have you recently introduced new procedures that are alienating these customers? Is there someone new dealing with these customers who might be handling them in a different style? Are there any common factors in the customers you are losing, ie are they all from the same background or buying the same or similar products or services?

You need to pinpoint exactly why these customers are no longer buying from you and the best way to find out is to speak to them. Also speak to the staff dealing with them. Once you know the reasons you can then put things right and take action to win back these lost customers.

Question: In the past we've had some poor comments about our service on the internet. We've now corrected these but once these remarks are on the internet they stay there. What can we do to overcome this?

This is always a difficult one, but you need to communicate very strongly through your website, and other marketing material, that you have listened to your customers and that you have now improved your services. Be specific; answer each negative comment or criticism by acknowledging it and then saying what you have done to address it. Send all your lost customers a newsletter or e-newsletter announcing the changes and offering them a special discount or money-off voucher to tempt them to return to you. Hopefully they will and will then post a good review about your organisation. Make sure you capitalise on any good reviews you receive since improving the service/product, and display these on your website, in your e-newsletters and newsletters, sales literature etc.

Question: I want to introduce a uniform for staff to help promote a strong corporate branding and make it easier for our customers to identify the sales staff. However, I am meeting very strong resistance to this from the staff.

In order to successfully introduce a staff uniform you need to first and foremost get your staff involved in this discussion. Be firm by saying that a staff uniform is going to be introduced and give valid reasons why. You might also wish to list the benefits of this. Say that you recognise that because they will be wearing the uniform it's therefore important to you to get their full co-operation and input into what will be the most appropriate and suitable uniform. Either get the staff together (if you have a small team) or take a representative from each department to form a committee on this. Before you can move forward with designs and options you might need to hear the staff's views (both for and against) on this to clear the air.

Rather than imposing on them what you think they should wear let them come up with ideas, which you can then discuss and refine. Input your own ideas gently as the discussion continues. Also, at the outset, agree a date when this will be introduced as you don't want the discussion to go on indefinitely. If you allow people to have their say and involve them you will eventually get their co-operation.

Question: I have some very good employees who have been with the company for some years. They are very loyal and hardworking. The problem is that our market has changed in the last few years; now there is more competition and our customers are more demanding. As a result of this we have introduced new working practices and new products and services which have been well received by our customers. I have, however, a couple of members of the team who are very reluctant to embrace these changes. As a result they are becoming a little difficult and obstructive. I don't necessarily want to lose them, but what can I do?

Change is difficult for most of us, but for some people who are motivated by security, and who by nature are more cautious, it can be seen as a real threat. It can make them feel insecure. As a result they lose self-confidence. Perhaps these staff members are worried they can't fully grasp the new procedures, or that it will take them more time to do so than their colleagues. As a result they could fear being made redundant, or feel they look foolish. Talk to each member individually and try to bring out their real concerns before fully explaining why these changes are necessary. It's possible that you could give them more time to come to grips with things or more support and training. Look at how you might help them through these changes; provide some on the job training, or perhaps coaching. But ensure that they view the training as support and not a punishment. Understanding that not everyone will react to changes in the way you feel they should is the first step to helping these valued employees to embrace it.

Question: As part of developing our customer service policy we are introducing an appraisal system for all our employees including managers and directors. The problem is we used to have a system some years ago but it slipped by the wayside as we became very busy. Now that the market is slower and more competitive in tough economic conditions we want to re-introduce it but are being met with a certain degree of cynicism by the staff. What can we do about this?

It's not surprising some of the staff are cynical about this. Having been there before and having heard all the well-meaning promises about why you should have appraisals only to see them tossed aside means you will have a job convincing them you are now serious about it.

Accept their cynicism and admit that mistakes were made in the past by abandoning the appraisal system. Give valid reasons why this was so. Reiterate firmly that you are reintroducing them and perhaps you can show how the new appraisal system is much improved over the previous one. Make sure you follow the guidelines for giving good appraisals and that the people giving the appraisals have training in how to do this.

In addition, I also recommend that all the staff have appraisal training on how to be appraised. It is, after all, a two-way process. This will help everyone to get the maximum benefit from appraisals. When ready, begin the appraisals and ensure that action from them is followed up. Once staff see the organisation is serious about appraisals and committed to them the cynicism will begin to evaporate.

Question: We are experiencing an increased number of customer complaints, in addition to which our profits are down and staff absenteeism is increasing. We've put out memos and emails urging staff to work harder and pull their socks up or they could risk losing their jobs but it doesn't seem to be working. What can we do now?

Firstly recognise that threats will not motivate your staff to perform better or provide better customer service. The reasons for more customer complaints and higher staff absenteeism indicate poor communication and motivation within your organisation. You need to examine the culture of your organisation, and move it away from a *telling* culture to an *involving* one.

Examine your communications strategy and remember effective communication is not telling, but is a two-way process and has to come from the top down as well as the bottom up. Have you got company practices that simply do not work and have been imposed? Look at the skills of your managers; do they know how to properly delegate and motivate staff? Are they fair and consistent in their approach to staff. Are you? Or are you and they continually bad tempered and aggressive? Also look at the workplace conditions; are they causing dissatisfaction amongst staff? Discuss with your managers how you can change the culture by improving communication and motivation and then put in place steps to do so.

Index